REVELATION

CATHOLIC & MUSLIM PERSPECTIVES

REVELATION
CATHOLIC & MUSLIM PERSPECTIVES

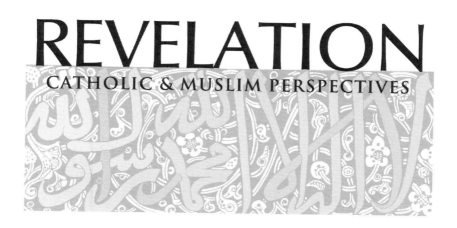

Prepared by the Midwest Dialogue of Catholics and Muslims
Co-Sponsored by the Islamic Society of North America and
the United States Conference of Catholic Bishops

United States Conference of Catholic Bishops
Washington, D.C.

Revelation: Catholic and Muslim Perspectives was developed as a resource by the Committee for Ecumenical and Interreligious Affairs of the United States Conference of Catholic Bishops (USCCB) and by the Midwest Dialogue of Catholics and Muslims. It was reviewed by the committee chairman, Bishop Stephen E. Blaire, and has been authorized for publication by the undersigned.

Msgr. William P. Fay
General Secretary, USCCB

The Word became flesh
and made his dwelling among us,
and we saw his glory,
the glory as of the Father's only Son,
full of grace and truth. . . .
From his fullness we have all received, grace in place of grace.

John 1:14, 16

This is the Revealed Book, which cannot be doubted,
guidance to the God-conscious,
those who believe in the Unseen, and perform the prayer
and give from what We provided for them,
and who believe in what was revealed to you [O Muhammad]
and was revealed before you
and firmly believe in the life to come.
Those are guided by their Lord, and those are prosperous.

Al-Baqarah 2-5 (Qur'ān 2:2-5)

Contents

Prologue

At a time of unstable international relations, of "wars and rumors of wars," it can only be a work of divine grace for people of faith to come together to do the work of peace making and bridge building. After years of dialogue in a climate of deeply felt friendship and hospitality, Muslims and Catholics have produced a common document on a central theme of faith: God's revelation to humanity. Since the Preface and Introduction to this document give the details of its inception, I would like to take this opportunity simply to express my gratefulness for the efforts of those who brought the task to fruition. In particular, I recall with affection my brother bishop Most Reverend Kevin Britt of Grand Rapids, Michigan, who was co-chairman of the dialogue, and who passed away in the course of the task at hand. May he now intercede for the continuance of this holy work.

It is my enduring hope that the achievements of the Midwest Dialogue of Catholics and Muslims may inspire others to pursue similar undertakings for the good of humanity in our times. I promise to petition our loving and compassionate Creator for the graces necessary, such that this work may embrace our world in light and peace.

Most Reverend Tod D. Brown, Bishop of Orange
Chairman, Subcommittee on Interreligious Dialogue

Preface

It is a great pleasure for us to present *Revelation: Catholic and Muslim Perspectives*. Participants in the Midwest Dialogue of Catholics and Muslims prepared this text by meeting annually from 1996 to 2003 under the joint sponsorship of the Islamic Society of North America (Plainfield, Indiana) and the United States Conference of Catholic Bishops (Washington, D.C.) through its Committee for Ecumenical and Interreligious Affairs. We now offer this text as a result of our work together.

Over the course of eight years, Catholics and Muslims from various cities in the Midwest region of the United States came together in dialogue. Most Catholic participants were the ecumenical and interreligious representatives of diocesan bishops; and most Muslim participants, already active in Christian-Muslim relations in their cities and towns, were acquaintances of their Catholic partners in those communities. In this way, by encouraging diocesan representatives to meet with Muslim partners in their communities, the sponsoring organizations engaged a broadly representative spectrum of experience and expertise in Christian-Muslim relations. After attending meetings of the dialogue, participants returned home with renewed enthusiasm to improve and increase Christian-Muslim relations in their Midwest communities.

The Midwest Dialogue of Catholics and Muslims offers *Revelation: Catholic and Muslim Perspectives* as a "working text" to be used in any number of ways by Catholics, Muslims, and others interested in relations between Catholics and Muslims. It is our hope that readers will use it as an introduction to our two religious traditions regarding the foundational topic of revelation. We had in mind especially Catholics in their parishes and Muslims in their centers as our primary audience for this text. Some might wish to prepare discussion questions for each of the chapters or the text as a whole or to develop a series of lesson plans or specific sessions on aspects of revelation or related topics. Others might want to expand on these chapters with lectures and a reading list on various aspects of Christianity and Islam. Still others might wish to detail further the moral and theological themes we hold in common by discussing our differences and similarities. All who have prepared this text hope that it will bring Christians and Muslims together in dialogue and study and will lead them towards greater mutual understanding and respect.

Thus *Revelation: Catholic and Muslim Perspectives* is primarily a text *from* a dialogue *for* dialogue. It marks an intermediate step in Catholic-Muslim relations in the United States, between the purely introductory level of dialogue and more advanced joint research. It shows similarities and differences and leaves areas open for further study.

As we came together each year, we did more than discuss various aspects of the topic; we shared our experiences and listened to one another's views and reflections on Christian-Muslim relations in our communities and in our contemporary world. We became friends, looking forward to our annual fall retreat and time together. We always allowed time to pray, each in our own ways, and were observers at each other's services of prayer.

By September 11, 2001, we had already met five times and were anticipating our sixth meeting in a few weeks. Our dialogue met as scheduled a month afterwards, and we discovered that it was the most satisfying meeting up to that point. We grew even more committed to our friendship and in the desire to bring our communities closer together.

These eight years of dialogue have been a remarkable period of spiritual friendship for us on this dialogue. We offer this text as a gift to all who wish to know more about this topic and to grow in appreciation of their Christian and Muslim neighbors.

We welcome reflections on this text and news about dialogues, programs, and other projects based on it. We encourage readers to contact the sponsoring organizations at the addresses listed below.

✝ Bishop Kevin M. Britt, Co-Chairman
Diocese of Grand Rapids

Ecumenical and Interreligious Affairs
United States Conference of Catholic Bishops
3211 Fourth Street, N.E.
Washington, DC 20017
seiamail@usccb.org

Dr. Sayyid M. Syeed, Co-Chairman
Islamic Society of North America

Interreligious Relations
Islamic Society of North America
P. O. Box 38
Plainfield, IN 46168
Isna@surf-ici.com

Introduction

Christians and Muslims identify themselves as followers and servants of the One God who communicates with humanity and is Lord of history. They refer to themselves as believers, because for them their faith is a response to God's revelation. They call themselves hearers of God's word and message, living their lives as proper responses to what they believe God has revealed to them and through them to all humanity.

Christians and Muslims are communities of believers who recite, pray, preach, and live according to their understanding of God's revelation. Christians and Muslims respect one another for their worship of the one, living, merciful, Almighty God who is Creator of heaven and earth and who speaks to humanity. Mutual respect allows Christians and Muslims to form lasting bonds of friendship and to cooperate in projects for the good of society, especially for those who are in great need. In doing so, they believe they are fulfilling the requirements of their faith as they each understand how they should respond to God's revelation. In an environment of respect, freedom, and cooperation, Christians and Muslims are able to enter into a truly interreligious dialogue in which they discuss their faith and through which they enrich and encourage one another through religious insight and practice.

A group of Muslims and Catholics, meeting annually for eight years in the metropolitan Indianapolis area to discuss the content, nature, and meaning of revelation, have prepared this working text. The group is an interreligious dialogue known as the Midwest Dialogue of Catholics and Muslims, organized and supported by the Islamic Society of North America (ISNA) and the United States Conference of Catholic Bishops (USCCB).

The Meaning of Dialogue

"Dialogue" is a word used in contemporary society with several applications. Several meanings of "dialogue" do not apply to interreligious dialogue. Some may use "dialogue" to refer to negotiations between disputing parties or to methods intentionally employed to instruct a person or group of persons about a topic. Some may use "dialogue" to refer to how they are going to correct a situation or to address an uninformed attitude. Some might imply by "dialogue" that they are going to express what is bothering them by getting it out and into the open. None of these usages conveys the important factors of an *interreligious dialogue*.

Interreligious dialogue is by no means based on compromise, whereby parties negotiate an agreement, each giving up a little, to reach a point that is mutually beneficial. In an interreligious dialogue, there is no attempt to reduce two sets of beliefs to one or to harmonize irreconcilable differences. While lively debates certainly occur during discussions, interreligious dialogue is not essentially a debate or an argument.

On the contrary, "interreligious dialogue," first of all, refers to a religious attitude that includes both commitment to truth and respect for freedom of conscience. Among the possible forms of interreligious dialogue is the dialogue of scholars and religiously trained specialists, like the Midwest Dialogue of Catholics and Muslims. In this and in other kinds of interreligious dialogues, one speaks what one believes to be true with respectful and careful attention to those who do not share with the speaker the same faith. Likewise, one listens to others say what they believe to be true. A participant in dialogue usually spends more time listening than speaking. Second, interreligious dialogue is distinguished by the topics discussed because this kind of dialogue includes both the witness of one's faith to others and the mutual exploration of religious convictions. Third, the environment for interreligious dialogue is distinct in that it serves holiness. Participants attend as members of their religious communities and maintain their prayer life and religious practices. Participants listen attentively and respectfully to the prayers of their partners in dialogue, and sometimes they prepare together interreligious services of prayer. An interreligious dialogue thrives in a "retreat environment," as participants share beliefs, pray, and assist one another in their shared desire to understand God's revelation. Fourth, among the several goals of interreligious dialogue are these goals that are distinctively religious: mutual understanding and respect for one another as religious persons; common action for accomplishing what one's religious faith considers to be true and good; spiritual growth and a deeper understanding of one's beliefs and those of another. These and other features of mutual exchange and sharing create a culture of dialogue.

In an interreligious dialogue between Christians and Muslims, the partners clarify for one another how they understand God's revelation. In doing so, their faithful response to God's grace that draws them together allows them to appreciate more deeply the many gifts that God bestows. Christians and Muslims know they have very great differences on matters of doctrine, and they do not seek to minimize these or to explain them away. Together they can seek to understand the mystery of the oneness of God and the meaning of the revelation that they revere. Catholic Christians and Muslims can agree that God calls them to interreligious dialogue and that it is under God's guidance that they come together to do the will of God.

This report on revelation resulted from such an interreligious dialogue. In the following chapters, Catholic and Muslim perspectives are presented on how each community understands revelation and how each seeks to live according to what they believe God has revealed to them. Thus, this report will offer both theory and practice for discussion and reflection.

The Midwest Dialogue of Catholics and Muslims

The participants in this dialogue are Catholic and Muslim friends and partners in dialogue from Chicago, Cleveland, Detroit, Indianapolis, Lafayette, Louisville, St. Louis, Toledo, and other cities and towns throughout the Midwest region of the United States, as well as members, consultants, and staff for the sponsoring organizations. Most are either imams serving Islamic centers or representatives of Catholic dioceses in the region. Some participants work for national or international organizations. Some are teachers, scholars, and theologians by profession; others devote much of their time to pastoral and spiritual guidance for members of their communities. The hosts are Catholic and Muslim partners in greater Indianapolis, and the sponsors are two national organizations: the Islamic Society of North America and the United States Conference of Catholic Bishops. Co-chairing the dialogue have been Dr. Sayyid M. Syeed, Secretary General of ISNA, and Bishop Kevin M. Britt, of the Diocese of Grand Rapids, Michigan, until his death in 2004. The first three meetings of the dialogue took place at Fatima Retreat House, a Catholic facility for prayer and spiritual retreats in Indianapolis; and for the next five years the dialogue met at ISNA's headquarters in Plainfield, Indiana. The first meeting was co-chaired by Dr. Shahid Athar of Indianapolis and Archbishop Alexander J. Brunett of Seattle, who at the time was bishop of the Diocese of Helena, Montana, and Chairman of the Committee for Ecumenical and Interreligious Affairs.

Annual meetings take place over a twenty-four-hour period, beginning with lunch on the first day and concluding with lunch on the second day. Participants find these meetings spiritually uplifting experiences and opportunities to learn more about their own and one another's faith. In spite of their differences in faith, participants strongly believe that Christians and Muslims can benefit from interreligious dialogue through mutual exploration of their beliefs and practices.

The members of this dialogue have shared with each other how they experience God's revelation in their religious observances and in the life of their communities. At each year's meeting, they attend one another's prayers, listening respectfully and offering prayers according to their own traditions. Since "the Word of God," as they each understand this expression, shapes their lives as Christians and Muslims, the participants in this dialogue not only have discussed this topic but have prayed from their scriptures in one another's presence.

The Work of the Dialogue

At their initial meeting in 1996, members of the Midwest Dialogue of Catholics and Muslims reviewed the recent history of Catholic-Muslim relations and shared their own experiences of dialogue. They decided to continue to meet once a year and to focus their discussion on how they each use the expression "the Word of God." At their 1997 meeting, they studied how this expression is used in their scriptures, the Bible and the Qur'ān, and discussed the different ways in which Christians and Muslims understand "the Word of God" and related expressions. They realized some important differences. Christians primarily refer to Jesus as the "Word of God" made flesh, while Muslims refer to the Qur'ān as the "Speech of God," that is, *Kalām-Allah*. For Muslims, the Qur'ān, which they often describe as "Revealed Guidance in Divine Words," was given to Muhammad, the Messenger of God, in portions over the course of his "Prophethood." The Qur'ān is ultimately guidance for living faithfully according to the will of God. Christians, however, believe that the message of revelation is ultimately God's own self, which is manifested through the person of Jesus and encountered through the preaching and living of the message of God revealed through Jesus. Muslims understand the Qur'ān as "the Words of God" or "Speech of God" because they believe that God revealed the Qur'ān verbatim to the Prophet Muhammad through the angel Gabriel (Jibrīl). Catholic Christians are more inclined to use "the Word of God" in the singular and first and foremost in reference to Jesus as the revelation of God made human. Christians might also refer to the whole of the Bible or to passages or readings from the Bible as "the Word of God," but this usage is not exactly parallel to how Muslims refer to the Qur'ān as "the Words (or Speech) of God."

At the 1998 meeting, Muslim participants showed how the Qur'ān is recited and used in their daily prayers. They demonstrated the style, skill, and art of recitation, or chanting the Qur'ān. The Catholics showed through both evening prayer and the celebration of the Eucharist how the Scriptures are prayed. They also gave instruction on prayerful attention to the exact words of a biblical text through the spiritual discipline known as *lectio divina* (prayerful or holy reading). Also at the 1998 meeting, the Muslims offered a detailed explanation of the *Al-Fātihah* or the opening sūrah of the Qur'ān that forms an essential element of all Muslim prayers. The Catholic participants offered an exegesis or explanation of the Our Father, or the Lord's Prayer, in the New Testament section of the Bible.

In 1999, participants broadened their study of scripture by discussing two papers, one on the major themes in the Qur'ān and the other on the major themes in the New Testament section of the Bible. They then concluded that they could prepare a resource together, with some sections drafted by each side and other sections drafted jointly. A drafting committee met a few months later to discuss the project in further detail and to assign tasks.

At their meeting in 2000, they discussed two prepared responses to the presentations of the previous year on the major themes of the New Testament and the Qur'ān. They also examined initial drafts of the sections in the present resource. The participants believed they could produce this resource by building upon their discussions and the good will and trust that had characterized their ongoing relationship in dialogue. A drafting committee was re-assigned and met a few months later to review drafts of the sections. At their meeting in 2001, the dialogue would be ready to discuss materials prepared by the drafting committee.

However, by the time of their October 2001 meeting, there were more pressing topics to discuss. All members of this dialogue, like everyone in the United States, were affected by the events on September 11, 2001, and subsequent developments. They needed most of the time for their meeting that year to share their reflections and experiences in the previous few weeks and to address together issues of violence and what the Bible and Qur'ān teach about it. The dialogue devoted even more time on its agenda in 2002 to a discussion of violence and revelation. The project on revelation was necessarily delayed, but in 2003 the dialogue returned to the task of finalizing this text.

The members of the Midwest Dialogue of Catholics and Muslims offer this working text as a guide and an example. They hope that it will inform Catholics, other Christians, and Muslims about one another's faith and teachings. They also wish that it will be used by neighboring Catholic parishes, other Christian congregations, and Islamic centers to bring Christians and Muslims closer together as neighbors and partners in their communities. The desire of the members of this dialogue is that this report will contribute to mutual understanding and good will and will serve as an example of what other religious communities can accomplish together. Most of all, they pray that this report will bring readers closer to God and to a deeper understanding of their faith in God.

CHAPTER 1

Catholic Perspectives on Revelation

Divine revelation comes as a grace to humanity, and the scriptures known as the Bible stand as the normative witness to that gift. Since some readers may not be familiar with the terminology commonly used by Christians about their scriptures, a brief explanation may be helpful. The Christian Bible consists of the Old Testament and the New Testament. The Old Testament is a collection of the revealed religious writings of the ancient Israelites. It has become common among scholars to refer to the Old Testament as the Hebrew Bible, out of respect for the Jewish people and their covenant with God. The majority of the religious books of the ancient Israelites were written in the Hebrew language. The New Testament is a collection of revealed Christian writings composed in Greek. All Christian communities share a consensus among themselves on the canon, or official list, of books of the New Testament, but they disagree on the full complement of books that are to be accepted into the canon of the Old Testament. We urge the readers of this document to explore further the complex history of the canon and the translations of Scripture.

Christians refer to the Bible according to the names of the books and the chapters and verses of those books. From the Old Testament in the Catholic Bible, this document will refer to the books of Genesis, Exodus, First and Second Kings, First and Second Chronicles, Isaiah, Daniel, Proverbs, Job, the Song of Songs, Ecclesiastes, Sirach, and Wisdom. (The last two books are found in the Septuagint, and therefore are in the Catholic and Orthodox Christian Bible; but they are not in the Hebrew Bible, and thus are not found in the Protestant Bible.) From the New Testament this document will refer to the four gospels (Matthew, Mark, Luke, and John), the Letter of Paul to the Romans, the First and Second Letters of Paul to the Corinthians, the Letter of Paul to the Galatians, the Letter of Paul to the Ephesians, the Letter of Paul to the Philippians, the First Letter of Paul to Timothy, and the book of Revelation. There are many more books in both the Old and New Testaments than those books to which this document refers. When this document refers to Israel, it means the ancient people of Israel, not the modern Jewish state.

Some theologians in the history of the church have been recognized as doctors or official teachers of the Catholic Tradition. Among these, this document will refer to St. Augustine, who lived primarily in North Africa from 354 to 430, and to St. Thomas Aquinas, who was born in Italy in about 1224, taught for a time in Paris, and died in 1274. The Catholic Church has had a series of ecumenical councils, meetings of bishops and church leaders from throughout the world, that decide major issues of Catholic belief and practice. This document will refer to the three most recent councils: the Council of Trent, which met from 1545 to 1563 with interruptions between the sessions; the First Vatican Council, held in Rome from 1869 to 1870; and the Second Vatican Council, which met in Rome from 1962 to 1965. These councils are cited according to the names of the documents that they issued, together with the chapter or section number of the document.

This dialogue represents teachings on the Catholic Tradition's perspectives on revelation and does not presume to speak for other Christian communities. Other Christian communions will agree to varying degrees with the positions expressed here and will frequently have different views.

Meaning of the Term "Revelation"

Christians believe that God has acted in a special way in the history of ancient Israel and in Jesus Christ to reveal who God is and what God wills for the entire human community and all creation. This revelation breaks into human life in surprising ways, challenges the usual assumptions of this world, transforms human awareness, and invites humans to a loving communion with God. For Catholic Christians, revelation encompasses the dynamic process of God's self-manifestation and self-communication as well as our transformation in God.

Revelation offers humans an intimate knowledge of God, and Christians experience faith as the gift from God that enables them to respond positively to this offer. Faith is more than intellectual assent; it involves the entire person in an act of surrender of the mind, heart, and will to God's invitation and call. Christians experience revelation in faith as leading them to salvation, to union with God. Concretely, revelation and salvation are experienced together as the divine invitation to share in God's own life and love.

Revelation is the radical nearness of God to human awareness, the transforming presence of the divine mystery in human life. While revelation truly discloses the reality of God and God's will, Christians recognize that God both is supremely intelligible in himself and also is an incomprehensible mystery to any created intellect, beyond the capacity of the human mind to comprehend fully or understand. In 1870 the First Vatican Council taught, "For the divine mysteries, by their very nature, so far surpass the created understanding that, even when a revelation has been given and accepted by faith, they remain covered by the veil of that same faith and wrapped, as it were, in a certain obscurity, as long as in this mortal life 'we are away from the Lord, for we walk by faith, and not by sight' (2 Cor 5:6-7)" (*Dei Filius*, ch. 4). Christian knowledge of God through revelation is always shaped by the recognition that the reality of God exceeds every human image, concept, or idea. St. Augustine warned his own congregation in North Africa, "If you have comprehended, what you have comprehended is not God" (Sermon 52, 16). St. Thomas Aquinas later commented that the height of our knowledge of God is to understand that we do not understand, since the reality of God greatly surpasses all our understanding (*De Potentia Dei* [*On the Power of God*], question 7, article 5).

Catholic Christians have traditionally acknowledged the possibility of an initial knowledge of God offered in creation itself. Because the Creator leaves a trace of the divine goodness, wisdom, and power in every creature, it is possible in principle for all human beings to come to a limited knowledge of God through natural human reflection. According to the book of Wisdom, "from the greatness and the beauty of created things their original author, by analogy, is seen" (13:5). In a similar vein, St. Paul wrote to the early Christian community in Rome that the power and divinity of God can be perceived in creation itself (see Rom 1:20). Catholics, like many other Christians, recognize that in practice this possibility is often threatened and obscured by sinful structures and patterns of thinking and acting. Christians believe that revelation is necessary for humanity to transcend the weaknesses and deficiencies of human nature.

In Christian discourse, the term "revelation" usually refers to a further disclosure of God beyond the order of creation. Divine revelation comes as a free gift of God, builds upon the natural capacity of humans, and elevates humans to an intimate knowledge of God that would be impossible without divine assistance. God freely and graciously takes the initiative in reaching out to human beings.

The Bible received by the Church as canon is the normative witness to revelation. It is both Israel's and the early Church's response to the revelatory movement of God in their lives. For Catholics, the written text is not itself the central focus but rather serves as the primary proclamation of the actions of God in the history of ancient Israel, in Jesus Christ, and in the lives of his early followers. According to official Catholic teaching, the center and fullness of revelation is not a book but Jesus Christ (see *Dei Verbum* [DV], no. 2).

Christians recognize the Bible as inspired by God, imparting the Truth for human salvation that God willed to be communicated. Catholics understand inspiration to be God's guidance of the authors of Scripture as they composed the books of the Bible. God worked through their own human experiences and abilities in the language and cultural forms of their time to convey the message of God's grace. The Bible is thus a profoundly human book, composed by a wide variety of authors over a period of more than a thousand years. In 1965 the Second Vatican Council taught, "To compose the sacred books, God chose certain men who, all the while he employed them in this task, made full use of their powers and faculties so that, though he acted in them and by them, it was as true authors that they consigned to writing whatever he wanted written, and no more" (DV, no. 11).

To communicate the significance of revelation, biblical authors used the literary forms of their time and culture, as well as the fundamental assumptions of ancient civilizations about the universe. Their writings were shaped by the criteria of ancient cultures and are not necessarily scientific accounts of historical events. For many Christians, and particularly for Catholics, divine inspiration does not pertain to the accuracy of historical or scientific information but rather, in the words of the Second Vatican Council, to "that truth which God, for the sake of our salvation, wished to see confided to the sacred Scriptures" (DV, no. 11). The biblical texts present the drama of the relationship of human beings to God in vivid narratives, images, and hymns in a way that communicates the saving Truth of God's love. The Bible does not offer literal history in the modern sense of the term, but rather offers literary narratives that express the significance of divine revelation in the lives of the people of Israel and the early Christian communities. The Bible is important for Catholics because it offers them the normative expressions of the revelatory actions of God. The Bible offers not an abstract definition or systematic theory of revelation, but rather *a series of inspired images and narratives* that present God entering into dialogue with humans, transforming human awareness and existence.

Most Christians hold the conviction that the original and definitive revelation of the new covenant came to an end with the death of the Apostles of Jesus, usually dated to the last years of the first century C.E. By the end of the second century, there was a practical consensus concerning precisely which books were accepted as part of the New Testament, as can be seen by the way in which Christian writers such as Ignatius of Antioch, Justin Martyr, and Irenaeus of Lyons cited these writings, and by early manuscript evidence. Responding to challenges to the canon posed during the Reformation, in 1546 the Council of Trent authoritatively defined the Catholic canon of Scripture, Old and New Testaments, in the decree *Acceptance of the Sacred Books and Apostolic Traditions* (Session 4, *Decretum de canonicis scripturis*, in Denzinger-Schönmetzer).

The Second Vatican Council noted that "God, who spoke in the past, continues to converse" with the Church, "the spouse of his beloved Son" (DV, no. 8; see *Catechism of the Catholic Church* [CCC], nos. 81-82). In the faith of the Church, the transmission of revelation comes through both the Bible and the Tradition of the Church, which "are bound closely together, and communicate one with the other" (DV, no. 9). The Church is open to continued growth in the understanding of revelation under the guidance of the Holy Spirit.

The Bible as a formally accepted "canon" serves the Christian community as a norm and standard of teaching on faith and morals. The "canonicity" of the books of the Bible specifically refers to the Church's conviction that these books contain the revealed Truth that is necessary for human salvation (see CCC, no. 107). The teachings of the Bible are interpreted in the light of sacred Tradition, which ensures that the content of the text is not subjected to misuse or misunderstanding down through the centuries of Christian history. In this way, Catholic Christians understand two modes by which revelation is transmitted: Scripture and authoritative tradition, which are bound together in a close and reciprocal relationship (see DV, no. 9). The living Tradition of authoritative Scriptural interpretation in the Catholic Church is called the *"magisterium,"* which is a particular charism of the office of bishop (see CCC, no. 77).

The Holy Spirit inspires the sacred author, illuminates the believer with the gift of faith, and enlightens the neophyte through the Sacraments of Initiation. The same Spirit gives the *sensus fidei* (the capacity to recognize the faith), the *sensum fidelium* (the consciousness of the content of the faith), and the *consensus fidelium* (whereby all the faithful agree in the faith). The magisterium is an office of authoritative interpretation by virtue of the work of the Holy Spirit in sacred Ordination and the spiritual grace given to the college of bishops and the pope.

Revelation and Salvation History

Since God wills all people to be saved and to know the Truth fully (see 1 Tm 2:4), salvation history is the drama of God's loving involvement with the entire human community; for Christians this drama is focused in a special way upon the people of Israel, the person of Jesus Christ, and the apostolic community. The Christian Bible presents a series of narratives, beginning with the creation of the world, centering on Jesus Christ, and concluding with a vision of the end of time. The Bible also includes a variety of other types of writings, such as hymns, prophecies, wisdom sayings, lamentations, letters, and poems. The biblical writings are inspired expressions of faith in response to God's revelation, shaped by the experiences of the ancient Israelite, Jewish, and early Christian communities.

Within the scope of the biblical writings, there is no one verse that completely encompasses the meaning of revelation for Catholic Christians. However, such passages as 2 Timothy 3:16 ("all scripture is inspired by God and is useful for teaching . . .") and 2 Peter 1:20-21 ("no prophecy of scripture . . . is a matter of personal interpretation, for no prophecy ever came through human will; but rather human beings moved by the holy Spirit spoke under the influence of God") are crucial for any Christian theology of revelation and inspiration (see CCC, nos. 105-107; DV, no. 11). There are a wide variety of experiences of revelation recounted in all parts of the Bible, from the primordial theophanies of Abraham, Isaac, and Jacob to the last book of the New Testament itself, the Revelation of St. John.

The actual text of the Bible contains a variety of literary forms that express the experience of God as it unfolded in the overall history of salvation. The Pentateuch or Torah, the first five books of the Bible, consists of four major traditions that have been woven together by the editors. There are two major histories of ancient Israel: one beginning with the Pentateuch and proceeding through a number of books to the Second Book of Kings, and the other consisting of the two books of Chronicles, which recount the same events from a different point of view. The New Testament presents four different narratives of the life, death, and Resurrection of Jesus. For Christians, there is richness in the variety of biblical voices.

During the second century C.E., challenged by those who wished to eliminate parts of the Old or New Testaments in favor of a more restrictive canon, the Catholic Church maintained the consensus, inherited from the Apostles, of using the entire Old Testament (primarily in the form of the Septuagint, the most widely used Greek translation) along with the books of the New Testament, themselves composed in Greek. In this way, the Church affirmed by its liturgical and doctrinal use of Scripture that the diversity of perspectives among the canonical texts was a more adequate way to convey the message of divine revelation than reliance on the viewpoint of one human author or tradition alone.

The biblical authors, each of whom was a member of the community of faith either of ancient Israel or of the Christian *koinonia,* are believed to have been inspired by the Holy Spirit to make use of a variety of literary forms to express the revelation of God in narrative creativity. Thus the biblical accounts should not in all cases be read as exact chronicles of historical events. Instead, they are often celebrations of the mighty works of God in creation and in human history, presented with literary sensitivity and considerable theological diversity. In addition, the historical experiences of the communities of faith continued to shape the text through processes of editing and redaction, themselves subject to the grace of inspiration. The primary purpose of the Old Testament revelation was to prepare the historical community of ancient Israel to bring forth the Savior of the world, Jesus Christ; the primary purpose of the New Testament writings is to proclaim (*kerygma*) Jesus Christ as Lord and Savior of the world. In a word, the message of the Bible is one of salvation offered universally to humanity by the grace of God conferred through the mission of Jesus Christ. This central message animates the Church's understanding of the entire scope of Biblical narrative.

The first eleven chapters of the book of Genesis set the stage for the drama of salvation with the accounts of the creation of the world and of human beings as stewards of creation, followed by the fall of the first humans and the widening circle of sin that envelopes and endangers human life. In the covenant with Noah, God makes a solemn pact with all humanity and all living creatures never again to destroy the world by flood (see Gn 9:9-17). This covenant is a concrete expression of God's loving concern for all human beings and all creatures. The later covenants in the history of Israel and the life of Jesus presuppose God's original universal covenant with and care for all creatures.

In calling Abraham to leave his father's home and journey to Canaan, God initiated a special relationship with Abraham and his descendants (see Gn 12:1-3). God promised Abraham that he would have offspring as numerous as the stars in the sky, and in response Abraham placed his faith in God (see Gn 15:5-6). The Bible views Isaac, the child of Abraham and Sarah and the ancestor of the people of Israel, as the child through whom this promise was fulfilled; but it also notes God's promise to make of Abraham's other son Ishmael, the child of Hagar, a great nation (see Gn 21:18). God promised to maintain the covenant with Isaac and his descendants; and God also, in response to Abraham's request that Ishmael live in God's presence, promised to bless Ishmael and make him fruitful, the father of twelve princes and numerous descendants (see Gn 17:18-22).

The covenant with Abraham stresses the gracious offer of God's promise apart from any human initiative. In later Israelite and Jewish history, this covenant would be closely associated with Mount Zion; it became central to the self-understanding of the kings of Judah (the southern kingdom of ancient Israel) and the worship of God at the Temple in Jerusalem. The covenant with Abraham does not mean that God is unknown to other peoples. Indeed, the account of Abraham's encounter with Melchizedek, who is not of the family of Abraham but who is a priest of God Most High, recognizes genuine knowledge and worship of God among other peoples and cultures (see Gn 14:17-20).

The central revelatory narrative in the Old Testament is the exodus and the covenant at Mount Sinai. In calling Moses and in leading the people of Israel from slavery in Egypt to a journey toward freedom in the land that God promised them, God demonstrated his concern for and commitment to the people of Israel (see Ex 3-15). The story of the dramatic flight and deliverance from Egyptian oppression, commemorated each spring in the Jewish Passover meal, has been a powerful force in shaping Jewish identity, as each generation experiences the liberation in their own lives. The Passover was also the source of the Last Supper of Jesus with his disciples and significantly contributed to the formation of the Christian Eucharist.

Where the covenant with Abraham stresses the divine initiative and the graciousness of the offer apart from any human merits, the covenant on Mount Sinai places greater emphasis on the human obligations that Israelites accepted in entering into this solemn relationship with God. The traditions of the two covenants, associated with Mount Sinai and Mount Zion, intertwine throughout the Hebrew Bible, complementing each other and at times critiquing the dangers of each other.

There are also texts in the Bible that do not refer to salvation history, such as the wisdom literature found in the book of Proverbs, the book of Job, the Song of Songs, and Ecclesiastes. These works explore the experience of the presence or absence of God in situations of everyday life (Proverbs), in great suffering (Job) or passionate love (Song of Songs), or in an intense search for wisdom and meaning in life (Ecclesiastes). While the sages of Israel were aware of the hiddenness and mystery of God, the mainstream of the wisdom tradition finds a revelation of God offered implicitly in all human experience. Later wisdom texts, such as the book of Sirach and the book of Wisdom (which are included in the Catholic canon of the Bible but not in the Protestant canon) correlate the universal saving and revelatory presence of God in all human experience with the specific events of Israel's history. God's Wisdom, personified as a gracious woman who is present throughout the entire cosmos, enters Israelite history as the Torah and "pitches her tent" among the people of Israel (see Sir 24) and guides the people from slavery to freedom (see Wis 10:15–11:3).

The center and climax of revelation for Christians is the experience of salvation coming from God in the life, death, and Resurrection of Jesus Christ. For Christians, the principal revelation of God is Jesus Christ himself. Jesus lived and died as a Jew and sought to renew the people of Israel. His ministry manifested the power of God breaking into this world. Jesus freely offered love and forgiveness to sinners and healing to the sick; but he also challenged the world's usual values, issuing a call for conversion and threatening judgment upon those who refused the invitation.

At the center of Jesus' teaching was the proclamation of the Reign of God: "this is the time of fulfillment. The kingdom of God is at hand. Repent, and believe the gospel" (Mk 1:15). In the preaching of Jesus, the Reign of God is an image of revelation and salvation, referring to the act of God's coming into the world in a new way, overcoming the forces of evil, reconciling repentant sinners, and forming a community of faithful believers. The proper response to the proclamation of the Reign of God is *metanoia*, a Greek word that is usually translated as "repentance" and that literally means a change of mind, a new attitude, a new set of perspectives and values. At the core of this new perspective is radical obedience to the will of God. The revelation of the Reign of God is offered freely to all sinners, regardless of what they may have done; but to enter and accept the Reign of God demands a conversion of mind and heart.

Instead of giving a technical, conceptual definition of revelation, Jesus described the Reign of God in narratives and symbolic actions. Jesus taught through a series of parables—brief, vivid stories that begin from the everyday life of first-century Jews and introduce the presence of God, often in surprising ways that overturn the expectations of the hearers. According to the parables, the Reign of God comes suddenly and unexpectedly, overturns the values by which people have been living, and summons them to new ways of thinking and acting.

The ultimate values for Jesus are the traditional Jewish commandments to love God with all our heart and mind and soul and to love our neighbor as ourselves (e.g., Mt 22:34-40; Mk 12:29-34; Lk 10:27-28). Jesus made it clear that the command to love one's neighbor extends across religious and ethnic boundaries.

Jesus revealed the meaning of the Reign of God in symbolic actions. Among the most dramatic of these was his table fellowship with tax collectors (who were hated as collaborators working for an occupation army) and with people labeled "sinners" (e.g., Mk 2:15-17; Lk 15:1-2, 19:5). Jesus' eating and drinking with these people was a powerful sign of offering them entry into the Reign of God. To those who were scandalized by his conduct, Jesus proclaimed, "Amen, I say to you, tax collectors and prostitutes are entering the kingdom of God before you" (Mt 21:31). Jesus offered people a new way of access to the presence of God built upon, but distinct from, the Torah-based mediation of the Temple and the priests in Jerusalem. After he healed people, he refused to become tied down to a particular site but moved on from one town to another, healing all those who had faith in God. Parables, healing miracles, and meals were central to his revelation of the love of God.

In his preaching, his healing of the sick, and his actions, Jesus challenged and undermined the systems of domination that imprisoned first-century inhabitants of Palestine. The gospel of Luke presents his first public sermon as based on a text of the book of Isaiah that proclaims good news to the poor, liberty to captives, and freedom for the oppressed (see Lk 4:18). Like the Prophets and sages of Israel, Jesus proclaimed a special concern for the poor and the oppressed, and he measured his followers' love of him by their treatment of those in greatest need (see Mt 25:31-46). By proclaiming that the greatest person is the one who serves, Jesus proposed a complete re-evaluation and transformation of the dynamics of *diakonia* (service) in Mediterranean culture (see Mt 23:8-12). For the master to serve his servants, even to the point of washing their feet as Jesus washed the feet of his disciples at his Last Supper with them, was to overturn normal social relations (see Jn 13:1-16). According to the gospel of John, Jesus did this as a symbolic action for his followers to imitate.

At the end of his life, Jesus went up to Jerusalem just before the feast of Passover, when a large number of Jews would have been present for the eight-day celebration of the deliverance of the ancient Israelites from slavery in Egypt. At that time, many would have hoped that a return of the "Reign of God" would enable the Jews to overthrow the rule of the Roman Empire in the holy land of Israel. Not all Jews held these revolutionary views, since the Jewish faith was formally recognized as a legal religion (*religio lecita*) by the Romans, with many advantages that favored a flourishing Jewish presence throughout the empire. Jesus himself did not call for a violent revolution. Rather, his message seems to have been directed against the more intransigent exclusivist views of some of his contemporaries. However, his symbolic actions, performed in continuity with the prophetic tradition of ancient Israel, seemed to challenge both religious and civil authorities. Ruling authorities at the time came to fear that Jesus' teachings on the "Kingdom of God" could be applied to political and revolutionary ends.

According to the gospels of Matthew, Mark, and Luke, Jesus entered the Temple in Jerusalem in this highly charged environment and drove out the money changers (see Mt 21:12-13; Mk 11:15-19; Lk 19:45-48). This symbolic action directly challenged the authority of the chief priests, who administered the Temple and collaborated with the Romans in the administration of Israel. A short time later, at the recommendation of some Jewish leaders, the Roman procurator Pontius Pilate authorized Jesus' death by crucifixion. This execution would have been part of the policies of repression used in Palestine against revolutionary movements in the course of the first century.

According to the usual calculations of history, the Jewish and Roman leaders would have expected the death of Jesus to be the end of his influence. The New Testament acknowledges that the followers of Jesus were indeed frightened, disoriented, and confused after his death. Contrary to expectations, a number of Jesus' followers and even one active persecutor of the early Christian community, Paul, began to proclaim that Jesus had been raised from the dead, had appeared to them, and had sent them out to spread the Good News. Jesus, who had proclaimed the Kingdom of God, was recognized as the Christ, the Anointed One or the Messiah expected by the people of ancient Israel. After his Resurrection, Jesus was believed in as the Risen Lord, the Son of God, the definitive revelation of God in history. Early Christians experienced the Reign of God, and the revelation of God's love coming in the death and Resurrection of Jesus himself, not as an outward political triumph over the Romans but as the decisive victory of God over the powers of sin and death.

The New Testament does not provide an eyewitness account of the Resurrection of Jesus from the tomb. Instead, the proclamation of the Resurrection is presented in a variety of narratives including the discovery of the empty tomb and experiences of the Risen Jesus by people who saw him, ate with him, and spoke with him after his death. These accounts reflect several decades of theological development of the original oral retelling of the post-Resurrection experiences of the early community (see Pontifical Biblical Commission, *Instruction Concerning the Historical Truth of the Gospels* [1964], nos. 7-10, in Denzinger-Schönmetzer). A key witness to the Risen Jesus is the apostle Paul, known in his earlier life as a Jewish scholar whose Hebrew name was Saul. His experience of the Risen Jesus occurred several years after the event itself (see Acts 9:1-9; Gal 1:11-24). Writing to the Christian community in Corinth in about the years 52-54 C.E., Paul handed on a tradition that had already become a fixed formula of faith:

For I handed on to you as of first importance what I also received: that Christ died for our sins in accordance with the scriptures; that he was buried; that he was raised on the third day in accordance with the scriptures; that he appeared to Cephas [Peter], then to the Twelve. After that, he appeared to more than five hundred brothers at once, most of whom are still living, though some have fallen asleep. After that he appeared to James, then to all the apostles. Last of all, as to one born abnormally, he appeared to me. For I am the least of the apostles, not fit to be called an apostle, because I perse-cuted the church of God. (1 Cor 15:3-9)

During the two decades between the death and Resurrection of Jesus and the time of Paul's letters (which are the earliest Christian writings to come down to us), the early Church confessed its faith in Jesus as the Mes-siah ("Anointed One of God"), the Christ, the Son of God, the "One through whom all things were made," and the mediator of a new covenant between God and all humanity. For Paul and other early Christians, the turning point of world history had already occurred in the death and Resurrection of Jesus. Followers of Jesus sensed that he was more than a Prophet or wisdom teacher. They experienced forgiveness, acceptance, and the offer of eternal life from him. At the end of the gospel of John, the Apostle Thomas would shape the later Christian tradition when he acclaims Jesus as "my Lord and my God" (Jn 20:28).

There was no sense of a division between being Jewish and being Chris-tian at this time. However, building on theological ideas already present in sectarian and mystical Judaism, the early Christians recognized the unique-ness of Jesus' own identity: "now glorify me, Father, with you, with the glory that I had with you before the world began" (Jn 17:5; see Jn 14:9-10, 20; and 16:28). In confessing the uniqueness of Jesus' identity came the parting of the ways between Judaism and Christianity.

Forms of Revelation

Prophetic

The Bible describes a wide variety of revelatory experiences. The central form of revelation in the Old Testament is the prophetic call (e.g., Is 6:1-13; Jer 1:4-19; Ez 2:1-8; Am 7:14-15). The prophetic call is a special gift from God and is not dependent upon prior human virtue or efforts; nor is it accessible through the ordinary experience of life. This call comes unexpectedly, and the person addressed frequently claims not to be worthy of the task. Nonetheless, the divine summons is not to be denied. The literary form of the prophetic oracle proclaims the word of the Lord and expresses the message God wills to be delivered, frequently condemning injustice and calling for repentance.

Sometimes extraordinary signs of nature serve as theophanies, outward manifestations of the divine presence. At Mount Sinai there was an earthquake and a storm, thunder and lightening, and a dark cloud and a loud trumpet blast to reveal the presence of God (see Ex 19:16-25). While the people were restrained from approaching the sacred place, Moses ascended the mountain to converse with God, and when he descended, there was a glow on his face (see Ex 34:29-31). According to one account, Moses and seventy-three leaders of the Israelites went up the mountain, saw God, and ate and drank with God (see Ex 24:9-11).

According to the First Book of Kings, Elijah came to Mount Sinai (also known as Horeb, the mountain of God) centuries later and experienced the same theophanies that had earlier been signs of the divine presence, but this time God was not in the storm or the earthquake or the fire. Instead, Elijah found God in the sound of a gentle breeze (see 1 Kings 19:11-18). After this the voice of God spoke to him. This marked a major development in the history of Israel and a turn to greater interiority in the form of the experience of revelation.

Wisdom, or Sapiential

The wisdom tradition of Israel did not look for revelation in special experiences of a prophetic call or theophanies in nature; instead the sages found God revealed in the experiences of everyday life. The book of Proverbs presents God's Wisdom as the symbolic form of God's revelation. Wisdom, personified as a gracious woman, is a poetic symbol for the ordering power of God in creation (see Prv 8); she plays at the creation of the universe, holds all things in the cosmos together (see Wis 1:7), and takes a special delight in human beings. In wisdom literature she is the form in which God seeks out humans and in which God wishes to be sought by them. She calls out at the city gates and invites humans to find genuine life and lasting treasures in her. God's Wisdom invites humans to accept her discipline, follow her ways, and find life, prosperity, and happiness. Wisdom is offered to all people. The wisdom tradition of the Bible recognized a true knowledge of God in other religious traditions and even incorporated a portion of the Egyptian wisdom text *The Wisdom of Amenemope* into the book of Proverbs.

Apocalyptic

Another type of literature in the Bible is called "apocalyptic," from the Greek word meaning "revelation." The book of Daniel presents revelation in the form of mysterious apocalyptic visions that come to Daniel (see Dn 7-11). He cannot understand the symbolism of the visions on his own and needs an angelic interpreter to decipher their meaning. Apocalyptic literature, represented by the book of Daniel, the gospel of Mark, and the book of Revelation, sees the world as dominated by powers of evil that are in rebellion against God and trusts that God will intervene to establish justice both in this world and beyond the grave. Apocalyptic revelation, communicated through mysterious symbols about an ongoing struggle between good and evil, comes as a promise of the vindication of the victims of history.

New Testament

All of the earlier forms of revelation in the history of Israel shaped the New Testament's presentation of Jesus Christ. There is an intertwining of prophetic, sapiential, and apocalyptic forms throughout the Christian scriptures. Jesus appears as a Prophet called by God the Father (see Lk 4:16-21), as a wisdom teacher who uses wisdom sayings and parables (see Mt 5-7), and, on more than one occasion, as an apocalyptic visionary who sees Satan fall from the heavens (see Lk 10:18) and foresees the end times (see Mark 13 and parallels). On another occasion, Jesus went up a mountain and was transfigured before Peter, James, and John, with a radiant bright light revealing the glory of God shining forth from him. Alongside Jesus appeared Moses and Elijah, representing the Law and the Prophets of the earlier Jewish tradition and conversing with Jesus in his transfigured state (see Mk 9:2-9).

The New Testament goes beyond all earlier Israelite and Jewish forms of revelation in presenting Jesus himself as the Word made flesh, the presence of God in this world. Every earlier form of revelation is applied to Jesus, but each must be broken open and transformed because Jesus is more than Solomon and more than Jonah, more than the earlier wisdom teachers and prophets and apocalyptic seers (see Mt 12:38-42; Lk 11:29-32); he is God among us (see Mt 1:23). The Resurrection appearances are the ultimate revelation of his glory and triumph.

Living the Gospel

Christians believe that what God has revealed through Jesus—the "Good News" or the Gospel—requires them as believers to respond in some way. Christians throughout history have tried to live the Good News, or

Gospel, with the knowledge that Jesus actively inspires them to do so. Christians respond to Jesus as a present and living reality and not as though he were merely a historical person who lived two thousand years ago. Christians believe that the "Risen Lord"—i.e., *Kyrios*—is *Adonai*, the God revealed to ancient Israel. He is among them now and will be until the end of time (see Mt 28:20). The Catholic Church teaches that Jesus is constantly made present in many ways: through the preaching of the Gospel, through the inspiration of the Holy Spirit, in the community of Jesus' followers (namely the Church), through the sacraments that are the special ritual actions of the Church, and in the lives of all humanity whom God has elevated through Jesus (see *Lumen Gentium* [LG], no. 16).

Although we often think of a "church" as a building—and in fact the church building is consecrated with a special liturgical rite—it is also the term for the whole People of God filled with the Holy Spirit. The word "church" comes from the Greek term *"ekklesia,"* which refers to those persons who are called (*kaleō*) out (*ek*) of darkness and sin to abide in holiness and communion with God through Christ in the Holy Spirit (see LG, nos. 2ff., 10). The visible Church is in historical and spiritual continuity with the Apostles of Jesus (termed "apostolic succession") through the integrity of its proclamation of the Word and celebration of the sacraments. This integrity is guaranteed by the authenticity of the Ordination of the clergy of the Church and by the judicious ordering of Church structure and life (see LG, nos. 8, 13-14, 18-29). The Church in fact is the community of all believers, living and dead, who have followed Christ. As St. Paul said, "now you are Christ's body, and individually parts of it" (1 Cor 12:27).

The sacraments of the Church are liturgical celebrations that make God present in the lives of Christians by means of God's grace. Grace, in Catholic theology, is God's loving presence freely given to human beings and awakening in them a free response of faith and transforming love. Catholics believe that the grace of God is freely offered to all human beings and invites their own free response in faith, hope, and love. In the visible signs and actions of the sacraments, God's gracious love becomes present and effective in the lives of the faithful. Jesus is encountered through the liturgical proclamation and preaching of the Word of God (i.e., selections from the Bible) in public worship. In particular, at Mass, the Risen Jesus is made present in the Word and in the Eucharistic Sacrament of his Body and Blood; communion with him brings about the nourishment of the Church, which is itself the "Body of Christ."

Jesus told his disciples that he would continue to teach them through the gift of the Holy Spirit: "the Advocate, the Holy Spirit that the Father will send in my name—he will teach you everything and remind you of all that I told you" (Jn 14:26). St. Paul testified that he personally experienced Jesus through the Holy Spirit, boasting of "what Christ has accomplished through me . . . by the power of the Spirit" of God (Rom 15:18). Paul went on to say elsewhere that the Spirit dwells not only in him, but in each follower of Christ: "do you not know that your body is a temple of the Holy Spirit within you, whom you have from God" (1 Cor 6:19).

Catholics experience the presence of Jesus in a particular way in the seven sacraments, which are rites of the Church that communicate his saving grace in a visible way. The Second Vatican Council taught that through Baptism Christians "are grafted into the paschal mystery of Christ; they die with him, are buried with him, and rise with him. They receive the spirit of adoption as sons [and daughters] 'in which we cry, Abba, Father' (Rom 8:15) and thus become true adorers such as the Father seeks. In like manner as often as they eat the Supper of the Lord [i.e., the Eucharist] they proclaim the death of the Lord until he comes (cf. 1 Cor 2:26)" (*Sacrosanctum Concilium* [SC], no. 6). When Catholics participate in sacramental action, they believe they are receiving the Risen Christ who offers them God's saving grace. For Catholics, these seven sacramental actions include reception into the Church through Baptism, the special reception of the Holy Spirit in Confirmation, the celebration of the Eucharist, the repentance from sin through the Sacrament of Penance and Reconciliation, the healing of mind and body through the Sacrament of Anointing of the Sick, the pledging of faithfulness to a spouse through the vows of Marriage, and the reception of the gift of God's ministry through Ordination as a deacon, priest, or bishop.

Christians are challenged to see Christ in others, since all people have been created in the image and likeness of God (see Gn 1:26). Jesus told his disciples that he is especially present in the "least ones," the poor and lowly of the world. When describing Judgment Day, Jesus praised the righteous for feeding and clothing the poor, visiting the sick and imprisoned, and welcoming the stranger, because "whatever you did for one of these least brothers of mine, you did for me" (Mt 25:40; see Mt 25:35-40). Knowing of Jesus' presence within all people—even the lowliest—inspires Christians to treat everyone with dignity.

Christians respond to God's revelation through Jesus by trying to conform their lives to his life as revealed in the Gospel. Jesus told his disciples, "Whoever believes in me will do the works that I do" (Jn 14:12). Through

New Testament books and writings from the early centuries of Christianity, Christians discover what the first communities believed and practiced in following the teachings of Jesus. To follow Jesus means to do as he did and as he said: to love God and neighbor, to serve the needy, to be willing to suffer when necessary, to forgive others, to be a source of healing, to oppose injustice, to reform one's life, to pray, and to share the Good News of the Gospel with others. These early testimonies and accounts instruct Christians in how to respond in faith to the Good News of Jesus. For example, St. Paul exhorted Christians to pray always (see Eph 6:18), to rejoice in the Lord (see Phil 4:6), to work honestly and share with the needy (see Eph 4:28), to be modest and sober (see Gal 5:19-21), and to persevere despite difficulty (see 2 Cor 4:8-11). Paul urged these early Christians to allow the Spirit to guide them and said that they will receive the "fruit of the Spirit": "love, joy, peace, patience, kindness, generosity, faithfulness, gentleness, and self-control" (Gal 5:22-23).

Christians of all ages have tried to live the Gospel both individually and collectively. Individually, Christians try to live the Gospel through daily moral conduct and also through the choice of a specific way of life that will help them follow Jesus. The Gospel sets forth a number of virtues that challenge Christians to serve others, to freely give their time and treasure to help those with material, spiritual, or physical needs. Christians are called to chastity, which means no sexual relations for the unmarried or for those who have taken the vow of chastity, and proper sexual relations for those who are married. They are challenged to be temperate, avoiding addiction to alcohol, drugs, gambling, food, or work. The Gospel calls Christians to respect the sanctity of life, to maintain just business and personal relationships, and to refuse to endanger the lives of the unborn, aged, disabled, or imprisoned. They are also to be servants of healing, bearers of reconciliation, and instruments of peace for all whom they encounter. Revelation calls Christians to give of themselves and to be willing to suffer when necessary for the good of another or for society as a whole. Christians seek to uphold the gospel values of service, chastity, temperance, respect for life, justice, peace, healing, reconciliation, and self-sacrifice in everything they do, no matter what life vocation they choose.

Christians also try to live the Gospel collectively, as the community that is the Church. For example, they organize efforts to take care of the immediate needs of the poor and sick through schools, hospitals, social service agencies, religious orders of women and men dedicated to service, and relief organizations worldwide. Through these agencies and other efforts, the Church also works to change unjust social structures. The Gospel also calls

Christians to be healers and a people of reconciliation and forgiveness. Finally, Christians try to live the Gospel by making public their views on current ethical issues and living by them. Today the Catholic Church serves as a witness against euthanasia, abortion, and capital punishment. Christians recall that Jesus drew attention to the needs of the weakest members of society, spoke out against injustice, and challenged the status quo (e.g., Lk 13:10-16; Mt 21:12-15). Likewise, today the Church, as a community of believers, understands that to follow the Gospel of Jesus means to demand justice for the weakest members of society.

The Catholic participants in this dialogue recognize that all questions that Muslims may have about Christian perspectives on revelation and other related themes raised in this chapter are not answered here. They hope that this topic and related themes have been presented so as to encourage further discussion and dialogue.

CHAPTER 2

Islamic Perspectives on Revelation

"*Islam*" is a word of the Arabic language that means "peace through submission to the will of God." Islam is the religion of more than a billion people throughout the world. The Qur'ān is the Divine Book, revealed from 610-632 C.E. to the Prophet Muhammad (peace be upon him and all the Prophets).[1] It is the basic source of guidance in Islam. The Prophet also explained the Divine Words in his own language and through his own practical example, and these are called collectively *Sunnah* (or the Tradition) of the Prophet. The Divine Book and the Tradition of the Prophet have been inspiring millions of Muslims, through centuries, to the path of peace in this world as well as in the Hereafter. In the Qur'ān, God calls people to the House of Peace (*Dārus-Salām*) or Paradise (11:25). To the believers who do their duty to God as well as their duties to their fellow human beings, as assigned by God, and who work for peace and justice in the human world, God promises forgiveness of their sins. And in the Hereafter, they will live forever in the House of Peace (*Dārus-Salām*), in the vicinity of their Lord (6:127). In this chapter, we will discuss the Islamic concept of revelation and its place in Islamic theology.

For Christian readers who are unfamiliar with the Qur'ān, a few introductory comments are in order. Muslims believe the Qur'ān contains the literal words of God as communicated in the Arabic language to the Prophet Muhammad. While the Qur'ān was revealed in Arabic, it also states that God sent Messengers to other peoples with his message in the languages of those peoples. The Qur'ān contains 114 sūrahs (divine discourses). Each sūrah comprises various numbers of verses (*āyāt*). Each verse (*āyah*) makes a point, and a verse can be a few words or more than one hundred words.

---

1 This is the general prayer Muslims make when they mention or listen to the name of a Prophet of God, and it is also their way of showing respect for these noble souls. There is a similar prayer especially for the Prophet Muhammad. Writing in English, some Muslims will place "(pbuh)" (for "peace be upon him") after the name of a Prophet.

The present arrangement of the sūrahs, which is followed throughout the world, is not the same as the order in which they were revealed. For example, the first revelation received by the Prophet constitutes the first five verses of sūrah 96. The Qur'ān was revealed piecemeal according to the needs of the Prophet and his followers, during his Prophethood (610-632 C.E.). However, the present arrangement of the Qur'ānic sūrahs was directed by the Prophet himself, under divine guidance. It was put together in a book form (Mushaf) during the time of the first caliph, Abu Bakr. The third caliph, Uthman, made copies of this Mushaf and sent it throughout the Muslim world. The sūrahs that were revealed prior to the Prophet's migration to Madinah (622) are called "Makkan sūrahs," after the city of Makkah, while those received afterwards are called the Madinian sūrahs. Whereas the Makkan sūrahs focus on right beliefs and conduct, Madinian sūrahs deal with the practical needs of a growing Muslim community as it encountered different situations. Most published editions of the Qur'ān indicate whether a sūrah is Makkan or Madinian.

The Qur'ān is the verbatim revelation from God in Arabic. Sūrah 12:2 says, "Behold, We have bestowed it from on high as a discourse in the Arabic language, so that you people may understand." And sūrah 41:3 says, "A Divine Writ, the messages whereof have been clearly spelled out, as a discourse in the Arabic language, for people of knowledge." All translations of the Arabic text are an effort to understand the meanings and message of the Qur'ān and can never substitute the Qur'ān, nor can they claim 100 percent accuracy.

The Meaning of the Term "Revelation"

We are using the word "revelation" for the Islamic term "wahy." The Arabic verb "waha" means "to put in the mind." The lexical meanings are "to inform someone of something which you keep hidden from others" or "to give a quick indication." However, it is very clear in the Qur'ānic usage of "revelation from God to the Prophets" that it involves God's putting some words in the heart of a Prophet, the meaning of which the Prophet perceives very clearly.

What Is Revelation? And Who Are the Prophets?

"Revelation" is used here for the Arabic word "wahy," which is a very significant Qur'ānic term. As such, "revelation" is used for those special modes of communication through which God speaks to the Prophets and Messengers. However, it is also customary to use "revelation" for the "Divine Words," which are revealed. According to the Qur'ān, for the guidance of the human world, God selects individuals of God's choice to work under direct divine supervision. A person so chosen is called a "Prophet'" (*nabīy*) or a "Messenger" (*rasūl*). Quite often the two terms are used interchangeably. But sometimes Messengers are understood as those Prophets of God who are given a new edition of guidance or a fresh Divine Law, as is the case with Abraham, Moses, Jesus, and Muhammad. However, the basic teachings of all the Prophets remain the same.

Thus, Prophets and Messengers are honorable servants of God who guide the life of their fellow human beings around them, in the light of the guidance that God has revealed to them. The Prophets convey the Divine Words so received to their people and also explain the Divine Words to them in their own words. They live this divine guidance in their own lives; and with the support of those who believe, they address the human situation in the light of the divine guidance. Noah, Abraham, Moses, Jesus, and Muhammad were Prophets and Messengers of God. Though the Qur'ān refers to many other Prophets, it does not mention the names of all of the Prophets. What is important is that all Prophets and Messengers of God receive revelation, and only Prophets and Messengers of God receive revelation. The Qur'ān does not appreciate any discrimination between the Prophets of God; one cannot believe some of them and disbelieve others (4:150-152). Muslims, therefore, believe in all the Prophets. They also believe that Muhammad was the last and the final Prophet of God, as was also clearly suggested by the Qur'ān and affirmed by the Prophet himself. This implies that there will be no more revelations.

Revelation and Inspiration

In light of the above, it should be quite clear that revelation is radically different from inspiration (*ilhām*), which a pious person other than a Prophet may receive. Unlike inspiration (*ilhām*), which a pious servant of God may consider binding for oneself, revelation alone is binding for persons other than the individual who receives the inspiration. In fact, all the addressees of a Messenger of God are required to follow the guidance revealed to their Messenger. It is so because the Messenger is receiving the revelation for the benefit of all of his addressees. Instead of communicating with each person, God speaks directly to the Prophet only. Another distinctive feature of revelation is its unique clarity. A Prophet of God perceives the verbal content of revelation so clearly that there is no possibility of any doubt in it.

God Creates as Well as Guides

The Qur'ān repeatedly declares that both *khalq* (creation) and *amr* (governance and guidance) belong to God (7:54). God created the world, step by step, through a systematic process, and it is God who, at all times, governs and directs the affairs of the whole universe (32:4). Thus, the world has a twofold relationship with God. Anything that exists owes its existence to God, and God has prescribed a path for it to follow.

The fact is that God not only has created the universe but continues to sustain and guide it as well. The Qur'ān discusses at length how God's creative activity and guidance are at work in various domains, for example, those that are areas of study for the sciences of astronomy, botany, zoology, and so on. Indeed, the laws of nature, including natural instincts of animals like the bees mentioned in Qur'ān 16:68, are all part of a system of guiding principles that God has laid out.

Forms of Revelation

According to the Qur'ān, human life is a different domain altogether from plants and animals. For example, Qur'ān 32:9 says of the human person, "And then He [God] forms him in accordance with what he is meant to be, and breathes into him of His spirit: and [thus, O mankind,] He endows you with hearing, and sight, and ability to think: [yet] how seldom are you grateful!" Likewise, God has given human beings the ability to distinguish right from wrong.

God has given humanity hearing, seeing, and thinking. Owing to these, humans are able to grasp religious truths when recited to them in their languages. They have the ability to see the phenomena of nature as divine signs. They are able to perceive in these phenomena the Hands of their Merciful Lord working for the benefit of human life. They have the ability to reflect upon human destiny and the purpose of human life. These abilities enable humans to understand the purpose of divine creation when it is explained to them, namely that through this life God, who alone is their Lord, is testing them and that on the Day of Judgment they have to account for their performance in this life.

Divine Guidance Through the Prophets

God promised to Adam and his descendants, "Get down all of you from here; and if, as it is sure, there comes to you guidance from Me, whosoever follows this guidance, on them shall be no fear, nor shall they grieve" (Qur'ān

2:38). This more specific form of guidance comes through the Prophets and Messengers, individuals specifically chosen for the task of guiding humanity to the straight path.

In Islam, acquired knowledge, no matter how extensive, is still insufficient to guide humanity. The knowledge, humans accumulate therefore needs to be supplemented by divine guidance. Sensory perceptions and their rational interpretations, on which humanity relies for the acquisition of knowledge, can neither comprehend the infinite nor perceive the divine will. Nor do these means allow humanity to determine and appreciate the reason for existence. That knowledge is the exclusive domain of the Creator. Guidance through revelation to the Prophets, therefore, fills this gap by providing information about three key areas for salvation:

1. Knowledge of the unseen (*al ghayb*)—This consists of knowledge of the unity of God, his attributes, his immunity from imperfection, the existence of the angels under his commands, and other unseen realities. Through knowledge, his servants know how to worship God and show him their gratitude. Humans on their own cannot know how to worship God and express their gratitude to him.

2. Awareness of the afterlife, the finality of divine justice, and the necessity of reward or retribution for one's actions in this life—This awareness inspires the believer to be cognizant of his or her actions, to behave responsibly, and to be fair and just in his or her dealings with others.

3. Recognition of the limits on human behavior—This knowledge assists humanity in separating right from wrong and thereby developing a discipline in their lives for regulating personal and social conduct.

Three Main Ways Through Which Prophets Receive Revelations

The manner in which God reveals his message to his Prophets is described in the Qur'ān: "It is not fitting for a mortal man that God should speak to him except by revelation, or from behind a veil, or by sending a special Messenger to reveal, with God's permission, what God wills: for God is Most High, Most Wise" (42:51). Thus, revelation can be conveyed in one of three modes:

1. The unique experience of *wahy* or revelation, through which Prophets receive Divine Words—This mode is best explained through a *hadith* (a report from the Prophet Muhammad) related by Aisha, where the

Prophet answered when a companion asked him how he received revelation: "Sometimes it is (revealed) like the ringing of a bell; this form of revelation is the hardest of all; and then when this state passes off, I have already clearly grasped what is revealed to me" (al-Bukhari, 3).

2. Spoken words, as if from behind a veil, so that one hears without seeing the speaker—This is illustrated in the way that Moses heard God's call from behind the bush (Qur'ān 27:8).

3. Words or speech through a special intermediary from God—The Prophet may or may not see the angel, but he does receive the communication in his heart. God sent the angel Gabriel (Jibrīl) as the Messenger to earlier Prophets as well to the Prophet Muhammad to reveal his message.

The Prophet and the Divine Revelation

Even this guidance from God through a Prophet has two elements: (1) a Prophet of God who recites, and (2) the revealed guidance in Divine Words. Qur'ān 2:23 makes this distinction in regard to the Prophet Muhammad: "And if you doubt any part of what We [God] have bestowed from on high (that is, revealed), step by step, upon Our servant [Muhammad], then produce a discourse (sūrahs) of similar merit, and call upon any other than God to bear witness for you." This passage distinguishes God's revealed guidance to a Prophet in Divine Words from what a Prophet communicates in his own human words. In the strict sense, this Divine Writ alone is called "revelation" (wahy), and sometimes "the Book" (al-Kitāb) is also used.

This revealed guidance in Divine Words received by the Prophet Muhammad is contained in the Qur'ān. Hence, the Qur'ān is verbatim revelation from God: that is, word for word from God revealed to the Prophet in Arabic. To consider the Qur'ān as the work or words of the Prophet is both blasphemy and an affront to Islam. The Prophet conveyed the revealed guidance in Divine Words, that is, the Qur'ān, just as he received it. As the final and definite revelation from God, the Qur'ān becomes the standard and criterion for all claims to religious truth. The Qur'ān is both the first and final authority and source of Islam.

Revelation and Salvation History

Throughout history, God has revealed his teachings, injunctions, and information about the unknown to special individuals specifically chosen to convey them to the rest of humanity. Qur'ān 7:35 refers to this general fact: "O children of Adam! Whenever there comes unto you messengers of your own, conveying My messages unto you, then all who are conscious of Me and live righteously—no fear need they have, and neither shall they grieve." The Qur'ān mentions the names of Prophets who are known to Jews and Christians:

> We have sent thee revelation, as we sent it to Noah and the messengers after him: we sent revelation to Abraham, Ismail, Isaac, Jacob and the tribes, to Jesus, Job, Jonah, Harun (Aaron) and Solomon, and to David We gave the Psalms. Of some apostles, We have already told the story, of others We have not—and to Moses God spoke direct—apostles who gave good news as well as warning, so that mankind after (the coming) of the apostles should have no plea against God: for God is exalted in power and ways. (4:163-5)

There Was No Civilization Without a Warner (Qur'ān 35:24)

Although accounts of several biblical and Arabian Prophets are given in the Qur'ān, there are many others that have not been mentioned. A recurrent theme of the Qur'ān is that there have been no peoples who have not received a Prophet from God of their own as a warner (nadhīr). A fundamental article of faith for Muslims is belief in the books that were revealed prior to the Qur'ān. Thus, Muslims believe that the Tawrah or Torah was revealed to Moses, the Zabūr or psalms to David, and the Injīl or Gospel to Jesus in the form of revealed guidance in Divine Words, and that their *essential* message was the same. The eternal principles of Truth within revelation transcend time and place and thus provide a message of universal significance to humankind. All the principles contained in these books are everlasting and are reiterated in the final revelation—the Qur'ān. The Qur'ān states, "Verily, it is We (God) who have sent down the Reminder [the Qur'ān], and it is We Who are its Protector" (15:9). For this reason Muslims are sure that the revealed guidance in Divine Words, in the Qur'ān, is fully preserved. However, they do not feel this certainty concerning other scriptures. Muslims believe that other scriptures did not preserve the original divine language. Their translated versions became mixed with interpretations and explanations that make it difficult to distinguish between the intent of the Revealed Divine Words and the human understanding of them.

According to the Qur'ān, before the revelation to the Prophet Muhammad, Prophets and Messengers of God were sent throughout the human world. The message was the same: God alone is the Creator, Sustainer, and Sovereign;

everyone else is his servant. He alone is worthy of worship; and everyone will, one day, return to him to account for their performance in life. By showing the straight way to God, the Prophets also became models for humanity. They sought to unify the divided human family into one community of God's servants. Thus, everyone is expected to have mutual respect and regard and to share their resources. The mission of making all humankind into one family of servants of One God only was necessarily directed against socioeconomic and political injustice, oppression, and exploitation in human society.

By sending his Prophets and Messengers according to his plan, God provided a gradual moral and spiritual development of humanity as well as bestowed intellectual growth on humanity through scientific and technological progress and developments in philosophy, literature, and the fine arts. God sent various versions of basically the same divine guidance and prepared humanity for that stage when no further editions of revealed guidance in Divine Words and no more Prophets would be needed. The Qur'ān relates in some detail relevant history and mission of Prophets and Messengers of God (see 7:59-177, 10:71-93, 11:25-103). With the revelation of the Qur'ān as a final and definite guidance, this process of revelation was completed. A basic tenet of Islamic faith is that both Prophethood and revelation from God came to an end with the death of the Prophet Muhammad: "Muhammad is not the father of any one of your men, but he is the messenger of God and Seal of all prophets" (33:40).

Revelation Given to the Prophet Muhammad

To understand better the revelation given to the Prophet Muhammad, it would be useful to trace the story of the first revelation as it was recorded by Islamic history using a collection of accounts from *Hadīth* and *Sīrah* (biographies of the Prophet). In the year 610, the Prophet started to experience divine inspiration in the form of dreams. These dreams imbued him with the desire to seek seclusion in the Cave of Hira, located near Makkah. There he would meditate and worship for many days on end before returning home for replenishment. It was there that one day he received his first revelation. An angel came to him and instructed him, "Read." The Prophet answered: "I am not of those who read." The angel then squeezed him firmly until all strength went out of him. Then, releasing him, the angel again said, "Read." The Prophet still could not move and repeated, "I am not of those who read." Then the angel took the Prophet and squeezed him again and made the same command, "Read," for the third time. The Prophet gave the same answer. Then the angel took the Prophet, squeezed and pressed him a third time, and then released him and said: "Read in the name of Thy Sustainer who hath created—created man from clot! Read! And Thy Sustainer is the Most Bountiful. The One who taught people with the pen, taught humans things they didn't know before" (Qur'ān 96:1-4).

The Prophet rushed out of the cave and down the mountain, flustered and trembling. All he wanted to do was to get home and away from this scary experience. Then, when he paused for breath, he looked up at the horizon and saw the most incredible sight of his life. There, filling the space between earth and sky, was the same angel who had confronted him in the cave! The Prophet turned around and again there was the angel, larger than the mountains and staring at him, saying that his name was Jibrīl (Gabriel). This majestic, numinous vision so overwhelmed him that he turned back and ran without stopping to his home in Makkah.

"Cover me! Cover me!" he cried, when he plunged through the front door of his house. Khadija covered him with a blanket. In the morning, Khadija, his wife of fifteen years who knew him to be a man of integrity, comforted him and explained that God would never let anything evil befall him. She assured him that he was honest and charitable and upright and that, if something was to come, it surely was not going to be bad.

She took him to Waraqah, her cousin, who had embraced Christianity. After hearing the Prophet's account, Waraqah said, "That [was] the Angel of Revelation whom God sent down upon Moses. O, would that I were a youth! Would that I be alive when your people drive you away!" Then the Prophet said: "Why! Are they to drive me away?" Waraqah said: "Yea. Never came a man with a similar assignment but was persecuted and if I survive to the day, I shall help you with all my strength." Waraqah died soon after this conversation (al-Bukhari, 4).

During this first encounter with the Angel of Revelation, the Prophet Mohammad surrendered himself entirely to the angel's embrace. Here the highest quality of Prophethood is manifested. The Prophet, when he receives the revelation, submits his own dynamic personality to such a degree that almost nothing remains in him but the faculty of reception. This probably is the most difficult task ever set before a human being. In the average human person, the impetuosity of feelings, desires, and nervous sensations overpowers and dims the purely receptive qualities and the ability to listen to the voice within or above. A Prophet is a human being filled with the consciousness of one's life and the natural impulses for action and self-assertion; and at the same time, a Prophet has a purely passive receptivity, endowed with nothing but the highest sensitivity and the power of exact replication.

The primary duty of a Prophet, in contrast with that of any other spiritual leader, is not to produce images and ideas born in his or her own mind. The Prophet's duty consists only in reading out of the unseen book of Divine Truth and reproducing its exact meaning to humanity without additions or subtractions. Therefore, the word "read," the first revelation to the Prophet Muhammad, ideally expresses the call to Prophethood. The Law of God, the Eternal Truth behind every perceptible thing, was laid bare before him, waiting to be understood by him in its innermost meaning.

Thus, it would be inaccurate to translate the imperative *"iqra'"* by "recite," instead of "read." "Recitation" implies delivery before an audience of something committed to memory; but at the moment of the angel's first appearance there was nothing as yet in the Prophet's memory and there was no audience. On the other hand, "read" implies the conscientious following and mental assimilation of words or ideas from an outside source. This, without doubt, was the thing required from the Prophet. At first, he was under the illusion of having been ordered to read actual script; and this he knew he could not do because he was not literate. But when the angel Gabriel conveyed the revelation, the Prophet understood, in sudden illumination, that he was ordered to receive the spiritual message of the Supreme Being.

The Content of Revelation

There is a great economy of language and thought in the Qur'ān, and the text as a whole does not contradict itself. Every verse (*āyah*) of the Qur'ān makes a point; however, the verses of the Qur'ān are not uniform. Verses serve different roles and functions depending upon the subject addressed. Some verses are reflections on divine signs; others give glad tidings or warnings. Still others state divine decrees or laws, while others explain the wisdom behind these laws. Since the Qur'ān was revealed over a period of twenty-three years to address specific situations, Muslim interpreters have developed principles for understanding how later verses expanded or even abrogated the meaning of earlier verses.

The whole of creation is replete with the signs of God, and these are presented to us through the lens of human experience. Therefore, there are three kinds of divine signs indicated by the verses of the Qur'ān: those found in the external world; those in the internal world of principles, natural laws, and even human interiority; and finally signs of God in human history. The first kind of divine signs are simple enough: for example, Qur'ān 36:33-35 speaks of life coming from the lifeless earth, which God brings to life in the forms of grain, fruit, and running water so that humanity may eat and drink and offer thanks to God. Qur'ān 23:12-14 states that in the creation of the human person, an embryo develops out of an essence of clay to form various complicated constituents of a living person—external and internal, physical and spiritual. Thus, God should be thanked as the greatest of artisans. The human person is a wonder to behold externally. Moreover, in the interior aspects of thinking, sensing, feeling, and so forth, the human person is also a sign of God. Returning to sūrah 36, numerous signs are listed: polarities in creation, the interplay of darkness and light, the orbit of the sun, the phases of the moon, the growth and decline of a human person's life, the clear discourses of the Qur'ān, and the order of creation as it relates to human persons (36-40, 68ff.). All of these external and internal signs of God call upon humanity to be grateful to God.

The signs of God in human history are both the marvels of human society and human ingenuity and God's action in human history in giving messages to his Prophets and Messengers. An example of the former is in sūrah 36:

> And [it ought to be] a sign for them that We bear their offspring [over the seas] in laden ships, and [that] We create for them things of a similar kind, on which they may embark [in their travels]; and [that,] if such be Our will, We may cause them to drown, with none to respond to their cry for help: and [then] they cannot be saved, unless it be by an act of mercy from Us and a grant of life for a [further span of] time. (41-44)

This passage takes note of human ingenuity to make ships and other means of travel that are signs of God's own creativeness. Thus, the technological advances of humanity are manifestations of God's action in human history, but the same is true of the life of every human person. For God wills the span of days for each person; and even when the threat to one's life is so great, one can be spared by the mercy of God.

The action of God in human history is also manifest in the sending of Messengers. Qur'ān 14:5-14 mentions the sending of Moses and the saving of Moses' people from Pharaoh. The passage also refers to the stories of the people of Noah, of 'Ad, and of Thamud. The unjust and corrupt deniers of Truth were destroyed, and their examples provide lessons for humanity.

Other verses of the Qur'ān convey glad tidings and warnings. An obvious example of this is the promise of the garden of Paradise for the faithful and of the fire for those who reject the truth of God's message (see 2:24-25). In Qur'ān 36:63, there is mention of hell, about which humanity has been warned again and again. It is God's will that humanity has been given insight to know right from wrong as well as a free will to choose right from wrong. The glad tidings are for those who use this insight and make a choice for what is good and true; then they destine themselves for Paradise (see Qur'ān 36:55-67). In these and other passages (see 78:21-36), one finds graphic descriptions of the rewards and punishments in store for the God-conscious and the sinful.

Certain verses in the Qur'ān convey Divine Laws. The following example mirrors passages in the Bible:

> And lo! We accepted this solemn pledge from [you,] the children of Israel: "You shall worship none but God; and you shall do good unto your parents and kinsfolk, and the orphans, and the poor; and you shall speak unto all people in a kindly way; and you shall be constant in prayer; and you shall spend in charity." And yet, save for a few of you, you turned away; for you are an obstinate folk. (2:83)

The divine decrees contained in this verse, to serve the one and only God and to treat other persons with respect and love, are the unalterable laws of God. These verses serve as divine assertions.

Woven among the verses bearing Divine Laws are verses explaining the divine wisdom underlying these laws. Several of these passages occur in sūrah 2. For example, verse 178 states the law of retribution, based upon equity and justice: that is, the punishment shall fit the crime. The next verse (179) explains that the basis for law is always an insight into divine rewards and punishments, as well as forgiveness and a provision for an ordered society. Verse 180 states that, before death, those who are wealthy should make bequests according to the good traditions in society and that these should be binding, for (as verse 181 states) "God is all-hearing and all-knowing." Verses 183-187 pertain to the specifics for observing the month of fasting, so that believers will extol God for his having guided them in the right way and so that they may render thanks to him. Verse 190 states that believers should fight against those who have waged war against them; but they should not commit aggression, for "God does not love aggressors."

The verses in the Qur'ān, therefore, are not uniform but follow several forms for conveying divine guidance. In each of these there is a message, and it is a message that should be lived. True piety does not lie in following rituals while missing the spirit behind the rites. The believers must live the faith through their just and charitable actions. These are the commands of God and reveal the will of God:

True piety does not consist in turning your faces toward the east or the west—but truly pious is he who believes in God, and the Last Day, and the angels, and revelation, and the prophets; and spends his substance—however much he himself may cherish it—upon his near of kin, and the orphans, and the needy, and the wayfarer, and the beggars, and for the freeing of human beings from bondage; and is constant in prayer, and renders the purifying dues; and [truly pious are] they who keep their promises whenever they promise, and are patient in misfortune and hardship and in time of peril: it is they who have proved themselves truthful, and it is they, who are proved conscious of God. (Qur'ān 2:177)

Revelation in Practice

There is a balance between humanity's absolute servitude to God and humanity's honorable position in the scheme of existence. Islam understands that the Creator is distinguished from the creature and, at the same time, recognizes that human beings have the most honored status in God's creation. Human beings are worthy to serve as vice-regent (khalifa) of God on this earth. Thus, the angels are ordered to bow down before Adam, because it is Adam's progeny who will take the burden of responsibility of acting as God's vice-regents on earth, a burden that the heavens and the earth declined to accept (Qur'ān 33:72).

Islam also makes an absolute distinction between the essence or being of the Creator and the essence or being of the created, between the station of the Divine and the station of his servants, and between the attributes of the Deity and the attributes of his creatures. There should be no doubt or ambiguity about this clear-cut distinction.

When the Qur'ān says there is no one like God, it means that nothing and no one can share with him in his Essence or his Being. God is the first and the last and the outward and the inward, which means that nothing and no one shares with him in his Being. When the Qur'ān says that "all that is on earth will perish, but the Face of your Lord, Majestic and Splendid, will abide" (55:26-27), it means that no one shares with him in his eternity. God will not be questioned for what he does; but all creatures will be questioned, for no one shares authority with him. As the Creator of all things, God does not share with anyone his act of creating. As sustainer of his creation, God grants abundant sustenance or gives it in scant measure to whomever he wills. No one participates in his sustenance of the world. No one shares with God in his knowledge, for "God knows and you do not know" (see, e.g., Qur'ān 2:216, 222). No one shares God's exalted station, for "nothing can be compared with God" (Qur'ān 42:11). When the Qur'ān asks, "Do they believe in partners who are supposed to have a share in God's divinity, who enjoin upon them as a moral law; something that God has never allowed?" (42:21), it means that God alone is the legislator, making religious laws for the people. And thus it goes for each and every attribute of God, the Most High.

The opening sūrah of the Qur'ān (Al-Fātihah) serves as a summary of the message from God: "Praise be to God, the Cherisher and Sustainer of the Worlds. Most Gracious, Most Merciful. Master of the Day of Judgment. Thee alone we worship and Thine aid alone we seek. Show us the straight way, the way of those on whom Thou hast bestowed Thy Grace, Those whose portion is not Wrath, and who do not go astray." With this supplication the Qur'ān begins. This is recited by the believer at least seventeen times a day during five obligatory prayers. Indeed, recital of the words of God constitutes a prayer in Islam. The Qur'ān forms an essential part of daily prayers. The motivation for prayer is the desire to seek the Truth and the desire to do God's will and seek the pleasure of the merciful and loving Creator.

The Qur'ān describes those who will benefit from the Divine Words. This appears in the opening verse of the next sūrah: "This is the Book which cannot be doubted, guidance to the God-fearing, those who believe in the Unseen, and perform the prayer and give from what We provided for them, and who believe in what was revealed to you and was revealed before you and firmly believe in the life to come. Those are guided by their Lord, and those are prosperous" (2:2-5).

The Qur'ānic goal is to shape a believer's inner as well as outer life: the outer life is simply a manifestation of one's spiritual life. Thus, a believer is supposed to purify his or her inner soul through belief in the one, and only one, God. Muslims who give witness to the Truth that no one is worthy of worship but the One God, who is the Lord of all human beings, are required (1) to witness that there is no God but Allah and that Muhammad is the Messenger of God (the Shahadah), (2) to observe five regular daily prayers (salah), (3) to spend oneself generously in God's way and to share with needy human beings, (4) to observe fasting and abstinence during the month of Ramadan (sawm), and finally (5) to renew their commitment to God by performing the pilgrimage (hajj) to Makkah. These are commonly known as the Five Pillars of Islam.

A believer's purity of character should be manifested in his or her conduct, whether in business life, political life, family life, or social life. Islam provides guidance in all those matters to ensure that the key concepts of justice, equity, and above all kindness and generosity are demonstrated in all aspects of one's life. According to the Qur'ān, some of the characteristics of righteousness, among several others, are "to spend of your sustenance, out of love for God, for your kin, for orphans, for the needy, for the wayfarer, for those who ask, and for the ransom of slaves . . ." (Qur'ān 2:177). A believer is generous and charitable, and he or she is humble too. His or her deeds are motivated only by the desire to please the Creator: "cancel not your charity by reminders of your generosity or by injury" (Qur'ān 2:264), that is, through words that hurt the recipients of one's charity.

The believer is expected to be fair and honest in daily dealings with others: "woe to those that deal in fraud, those who, when they have to receive by measure from men, exact full measure, but when they have to give my measure, or weight to them, give less than due" (Qur'ān 83:1-3). He or she believes in human equality and brotherhood and respects diversity: "O mankind! We created you from a single pair of a male and female, and made you into nations and tribes that you may know each other. Verily the most honored among you in the sight of God is the most righteous of you" (Qur'ān 59:13).

The pursuit of God's favor should not promote self-righteousness. A Muslim may not impose his beliefs upon others: "there is no compulsion in religion" (Qur'ān 2:256). On the contrary, the Qur'ān enjoins respect for the houses of worship of other religions.

The Qur'ān reserves special respect for the "People of the Book," namely Jews and Christians. It even goes on to prescribe a framework for dialogue with the People of the Book: "say, We believe in the Revelation that has come down to us and in that which came to you; our God and your God, is One; and it is to Him we bow in submission and peace" (29:46).

The Muslim participants in this dialogue recognize that all questions that their Christian friends may have about Islamic perspectives on revelation and other related themes raised in this chapter are not fully answered here. They hope that this topic and related themes have been presented in such a way so as to encourage further discussion and dialogue between Christians and Muslims.

CHAPTER 3

Scriptural Themes: Muslim and Catholic Responses

The Muslim and Catholic perspectives on revelation set forth in the two preceding chapters provide a basis for further reflection upon both the similarities and the differences between the Muslim and Catholic traditions. In this chapter we acknowledge the important differences between our traditions, and we also examine and cherish the many values that we hold in common. Muslims agree with many of the perspectives and values taught by Jesus, presented and explained by the Catholic Church, despite the fact that Muslims do not see Jesus as divine. For its part, the Catholic Tradition affirms and accepts many of the teachings of the Qur'ān, though the significance of these themes for Catholics is often different because of the distinctive context of Catholic faith and practice. We will note areas of agreement, and we will also examine areas where Muslims and Catholics disagree in the hope that we can learn together from both our similarities and our differences.

Muslim Perspectives on Biblical Revelation

Muslims acknowledge that God gave revelation to important figures in the history of the people of Israel, including Jesus. Muslims believe that God revealed guidance, known as Tawrāh (or Torah), to Moses; the Zabūr (or psalms), to David; and the Injīl (or Gospel), to Jesus. However, Muslims believe that the current Bible in use by Jews and Christians does not preserve the original message of these revelations with complete accuracy.

Muslims revere and honor Jesus, and they affirm the New Testament's portrait of him as a Messenger and Prophet, a miracle worker who healed people, challenged the Jewish and Roman leaders of his time, and offered forgiveness, healing, and reconciliation to all. Muslims recognize with appreciation that Jesus challenged the world's predominant values, issuing a call for repentance and threatening judgment upon those who refused the invitation. Muslims also cherish Jesus' proclamation of God's special concern for the poor and the oppressed and his standard of measuring his followers' love of him by their treatment of those in greatest need.

In a passage that is similar to one in the gospel of Luke (Lk 1:26-38), the Qur'ān teaches that an angel appeared to Mary and announced to her the gift of a blessed Son even though she was a virgin (19:16-21). Following the Qur'ān, Muslims recognize Jesus as a great Messenger who was appointed to the children of Israel and who healed the blind and lepers and raised the dead by God's power. The Qur'ān also presents narratives of actions of Jesus that are not found in the four canonical Christian gospels, such as making a bird out of clay and praying to God to send a table with food for a great festival for his disciples (see Qur'ān 5:110-115).

According to the Qur'ān, Jesus confirmed that which was brought by Moses by making the religious Law more flexible and removing some of its restrictions. The Qur'ān teaches that there was a point when Jesus felt some frustration because, even after he had performed many miracles, some Jews said, "This is nothing but evident magic." When Jesus found disbelief on their part, he said, "Who will be my helpers to do the work of God?" He received two different responses from his listeners. The first came from those disciples who said, "We are God's helpers. We believe in God. We surrender to Him." The second response came from the unbelievers, who planned to kill Jesus (Qur'ān 5:111-113).

The accounts of the death of Jesus constitute one point where the Muslim tradition differs from Christian understandings. For Christians, the death of Jesus is a historical event that became one of the most important themes in the New Testament and later Christian literature. The Qur'ān, however, teaches,

> They said (in boast) we killed Christ Jesus, the son of Mary, the Messenger of God, but they killed him not, nor crucified him, but so it was made to appear to them and those who differ in this matter are themselves skeptical about it, and they do not have a sure knowledge but only follow conjecture and they did not kill him not for sure. Rather, God raised him up unto Himself and God is Almighty and Wise. (4:157-158)

According to the Qur'ān, Jesus was dealing with people who had already rejected God's guidance and killed the Messengers of God. They had also made false charges against a righteous woman, Mary, who was chosen by God to be the mother of Jesus.

Catholic Perspectives on Qur'ānic Themes

Catholic Christians acknowledge and respect many truths found in the Qur'ān and also esteem the way in which Muslims have experienced God's presence in and through its message. Many of the central teachings of the Qur'ān are important to Catholics as well; and so Catholics can rejoice in the positive benefits that the message of the Qur'ān has brought to countless people.

According to the Qur'ān, Muhammad is the last Prophet, and the divine message given to him is the final revelation. Catholics have a similar belief concerning Jesus, namely that the revelation of God in Jesus is the final public revelation from God in history and that no more Prophets are to be expected before the Second Coming of Jesus Christ at the end of time. Though Catholics may respect many teachings of the Qur'ān, they nonetheless do not see the Qur'ān as a distinct supernatural divine revelation.

For Muslims, faith in One God and one's total surrender to God is called "Islam." According to God, only one way of life is valid, and this is submission to God (Qur'ān 3:19). The term "muslim" means one who submits to God. Catholics, like other Christians, also stress the central importance of faith as reception of God's revelation and submission to God. The Qur'ān calls humans to submit their wills to God; in a similar way, Jesus taught his followers to pray to God, "Your will be done" (Mt 6:10).

Catholics see the core of this submission as a relationship of love. The chief commandment according to Jesus is to love God with one's whole heart and soul and mind and strength (see Mk 12:30; cf. Qur'ān 3:31). Catholics acknowledge that the patriarchs and Prophets of ancient Israel taught the same message. For example, in the book of Deuteronomy, Moses teaches the commandment to love God with one's entire being (see 6:5). Catholics can agree with the Qur'ān that Jesus and the patriarchs and Prophets of ancient Israel could be called "muslims" in the sense of being persons who submitted their mind and hearts and wills to God and called others to do the same.

The Qur'ān calls attention to the natural order of the universe and the laws of creation as signs of God's creative power (3:191). Catholics agree with the Qur'ān that we can learn about God through attention to the entire universe, especially its structure and order and beauty. St. Paul wrote to the Church in Rome, "Ever since the creation of the world, his invisible attributes of eternal power and divinity have been able to be understood and perceived through what he has made" (Rom 1:20). The book of Wisdom in the Catholic canon of the Old Testament (a Jewish work written in Alexandria, Egypt, shortly before the time of Jesus) proclaims, "For from the greatness and the beauty of created things their original author, by analogy, is seen" (13:5). The book of Wisdom also stresses the order and goodness of creation (see 7:13-22). Like the Qur'ān, the psalms call attention to the beauty of the heavens as proclaiming the glory of God: "the heavens declare the glory of God; / the sky proclaims its builder's craft" (Ps 19:2; cf. Qur'ān 17:44).

Catholics also agree with the Qur'ān that humans have a central role in the plan of creation (see Qur'ān 91:7-10). The knowledge of God offered in creation imposes a special responsibility upon human beings to honor and worship God as Creator and not to place their ultimate faith in any creature. For Catholics and Muslims alike, the tragedies of human history, rooted in idolatry, follow from the failure of humans to acknowledge the beauty and goodness of God that is manifested in creation (see Wis 13:1-9; Rom 1:18-32).

The Qur'ān's call to use one's mind to think about creation (3:191) also resonates deeply with the Bible and the Catholic Tradition. The wisdom tradition of ancient Israel, especially as represented by the books of Proverbs, Sirach, and Wisdom, teaches humans to reflect carefully and attentively on creation, to perceive the patterns of experience, and to understand the order implanted by God. Later Christians often reflected on the goodness and beauty of creation as a means of knowing God. St. Francis of Assisi, a thirteenth-century Italian saint, delighted in the creatures that God had made and prayed that God would be praised through them. St. Bonaventure, a thirteenth-century Franciscan friar and theologian, described Francis of Assisi's relationship to God:

> Aroused by all things to the love of God, he [Francis] rejoiced in all the works of the Lord's hands and from these joy-producing manifestations he rose to their life-giving principle and cause. In beautiful things he saw Beauty itself and through His vestiges imprinted on creation he followed his Beloved everywhere, making from all things a ladder by which he could climb up and embrace Him who is utterly desirable. With a feeling of unprecedented devotion he savored in each and every creature—as in so many rivulets—that Goodness which is their fountain-source. And he perceived a heavenly harmony in the consonance of powers and activities God has given them, and like the prophet David sweetly exhorted them to praise the Lord. (*The Life of St. Francis*, chapter 9, section 1)

One significant difference in attitudes toward creation is that Christians see the Word of God, which is incarnate in Jesus, as the *mediator* of creation. An early Christian hymn quoted in the Letter of Paul to the Colossians states of Christ,

> He is the image of the invisible God,
>   the firstborn of all creation.
> For in him were created all things in heaven and on earth,
>   the visible and the invisible,
>   whether thrones or dominions or principalities or powers;
>   all things were created through him and for him.
> He is before all things,
>   and in him all things hold together.
>   (Col 1:15-17; cf. Jn 1:3-4 and Heb 1:2-3)

Because Islam emphasizes that God creates everything by his command "to be," Muslims believe that there is no *mediator* between the Creator and creation.

The message of the Qur'ān contains many principles that Christians can accept. Like the Qur'ān, the Christian Bible, in both the Old and New Testaments, sets forth principles for reforming both individuals and society as a whole; it also addresses all humans, not simply a privileged class of political or religious leaders. While the Old Testament addressed the people of Israel in a unique way, the message of the New Testament, and thus of the Christian Bible as a whole, is clearly intended for all humanity. Like the message of the Qur'ān, the message of the Christian Bible uses a human medium in a particular time and place as a starting point. The Bible, again like the Qur'ān, addresses humans with regard to the ultimate success or failure of their lives in relationship to God.

The Bible further agrees with the Qur'ān in stressing individual responsibility in shaping the course of individual and social life. The Qur'ān has a universal audience—all humankind is to hear its message (49:13). The Prophets of Israel expressed the hope that all peoples would come to know and worship the One God (e.g., see Is 55). All people, not only Jews, were to be welcomed (e.g., Is 55:3-7). According to the gospel of Matthew, after the Resurrection Jesus sent his disciples forth to all nations to proclaim the Good News of salvation (see Mt 28:19).

The Qur'ān discusses the creation of Adam and Eve (2:30ff.), but it strongly rejects a doctrine of original sin (6:164). Catholic perspectives on this topic are based on the narrative of the fall of Adam and Eve in Genesis 3 and on St. Paul's discussion of Adam and Christ in his Letter to the Romans. Catholics today take the account of Adam and Eve in Genesis chapter 3 not as a literal, historical event but instead as a symbolic narrative that presents a profound truth about human existence. Catholics believe that human beings receive a nature that is weakened and damaged by the effects of original sin. This results in the darkening of our intellect and the weakening of our will, so that it is more difficult for us to know the good and to do it. According to Catholic teaching, the effects of original sin are never completely overcome in this life; something is awry with human nature, leading to the repeated tragedies of history.

Catholics agree with the Qur'ān on the importance of both justice and mercy (cf. Qur'ān 57:25, 76:8). The Bible repeatedly calls for justice in both personal and societal relationships. The Qur'ān calls Muslims to forgive those who have wronged them (3:134). Jesus made his followers' willingness to forgive others the measure for God's forgiveness of them: "stop judging, that you may not be judged. For as you judge, so will you be judged, and the measure with which you measure will be measured out to you" (Mt 7:1-2). Catholics strongly concur with Muslims that the family is the nucleus, the center of society, and is of great importance for human and religious development. Catholics also agree with the Qur'ān that believers have an obligation to provide for the poor. A society that practices injustice or that neglects the needs of the poor is abhorrent to God. Both the Bible and the Qur'ān view wealth, honestly earned and responsibly used, as a gift from God. But this gift brings with it responsibilities, including the care of those in need.

Concerning Judgment Day, the Christian tradition again shares many of the teachings of the Qur'ān (cf. 99:1ff.). Like Muslims, Catholics believe that each individual will be judged by God after death and held accountable for the decisions made in this world. Together with Muslims, Catholics also believe that each individual will come to a clear awareness of his or her conduct in life. Both traditions agree that before God there is no place to hide, and all self-deceptions are ended.

Muslim and Catholic Perspectives in Dialogue

In contrast to the Muslim belief that Jesus was not crucified, Catholics, like all contemporary Christians, believe that Jesus was crucified under the authority of the Roman procurator Pontius Pilate and that he truly died. Other ancient writers who were not Christian agree on this point. A passage in the work of Flavius Josephus, a Jewish first-century author, writing in the years 93-94, attests that Jesus was crucified by Pilate (*The Antiquities* 18.3.3); and the Roman historian Tacitus, writing at the beginning of the second century C.E., also reports that Christ was executed by the procurator Pontius Pilate (*Annals* 15.44).

The death and Resurrection of Jesus are at the center of the New Testament and of Christian faith. Catholics believe that Jesus truly died for the salvation of the world and that he was raised from the dead, appeared to many of his followers, and ascended body and soul into heaven, where he sits at the right hand of God the Father until the Last Judgment. These events are God's decisive action in redeeming the world.

The most important theological differences between Catholics and Muslims concern the Trinity and the divinity of Jesus. The gospel of Matthew states that Jesus will be known as "'Emmanuel, which means 'God with us'" (1:23), and the disciple Thomas in the gospel of John acclaims the Risen Jesus as "my Lord and my God" (Jn 20:28). These passages shaped Christian worship of Jesus as divine (*lex orandi, lex credendi*). The Islamic doctrine of *Tawhīd* (worship of One God) is expressed in Sūrah Ikhlās, which is sūrah 112 of the Qur'ān: "Say: It is God, the One and Only; God, the Self-Sufficient on Whom everything depends; He begets not, nor is He begotten; and there is none like unto Him." Muslims believe that to attribute divine power or divinity to any being other than God is to commit *shirk*, associating a partner with God. For Muslims, since God is the only Divine Being, no one shares any divinity with God. Likewise, divinity is indivisible.

The Qur'ān describes Jesus as Sign of God, Word of God, Spirit of God, Servant of God, Messenger of God, but also as one who is fully human and the son of Mary. The Qur'ān says, "The similitude of Jesus before God is as that of Adam. God created Adam from dust then said to him 'Be' and he was" (3:59). Therefore, Jesus was born without a human father as Adam was also born. About Jesus, the Qur'ān says that he is the Word of God that God cast into Mary (4:171).

The Qur'ān also describes a conversation between God and Jesus that apparently will happen on the Day of Judgment. God will say to Jesus, "Did you tell people to take you and your mother as gods besides God?" He will glorify the Almighty God and say,

> It is not my place to say what I have no right to say. If I had said such a thing, you would know it. You know what is in me, but I do not know what is in you. Verily you are the Knower of unseen things. I told them what you told me, 'Worship God, my Lord and your Lord,' and I was a witness over them while I was among them and when you took me up, You were the watcher over them and You are witness of everything. (5:116-117)

For Muslims, the issue of the Trinity is not only a theological problem but also a religious question. Muslims do not believe it can be coherently shown that God ever becomes incarnate in any form. The embodiment of God in any form leads towards idolatry and negates the transcendence of God.

Catholics believe that Jesus was not merely a Prophet called by God but was the Incarnation of God in this world. Unlike Muslims, Catholics do not believe that a divinely written or revealed book was given to Jesus; rather, Jesus possessed the full knowledge of God the Father and shared this knowledge with his disciples insofar as they could receive it. For Catholics, Jesus was truly human, like us in all things except sin; and he was also truly divine, equal to God the Father in every respect. According to the Catholic faith, Jesus is one person who has both a human nature, which is mortal, and a divine nature, which is eternal. When Jesus died on the cross, he died as a man, but this did not mean the death of his eternal divine nature.

In light of their belief in the Incarnation of God in Jesus Christ, Catholic Christians understand God as triune, one divine Essence, which is shared fully by three equal divine Persons: Father, Son, and Holy Spirit. The perfect unity of the divine Persons is not compromised by the distinctions among them. God the Father is the origin of the other Persons and shares all knowledge, wisdom, power, goodness, beauty, and love fully with God the Son in an eternal relationship. According to Catholic belief, the Father and the Son together are the source of the Holy Spirit, which is the bond of love flowing mutually between them. The Trinity expresses itself in the work of creating the universe and of redeeming and sanctifying human beings. All divine activities toward the world come from the Father through the Son and are *activated and perfected* by the Holy Spirit. God the Father sends the Son and the Spirit into the world to be present in a new way in Jesus and in the life of the Church. The Father is the ultimate origin; the Son is the perfect image and expression of the Father who makes the Father known to human beings; the Spirit is the power of God that enables Christians to accept Jesus as the revelation of God the Father.

In the late fourth century of the Christian era, St. Basil the Great compared the Holy Spirit to the light in which we see objects; the light itself usually remains unnoticed, but it allows us to receive the gift of God's revelation and grace. Basil noted that the human understanding of numbers is in no way adequate for understanding the Trinity: "the Unapproachable One is beyond numbers" (*On the Holy Spirit*, 71). In other words, he wrote, "We have never to this day heard of a second God" (71).

When considering significant theological difference between Muslims and Christians, it should be remembered that there are many internal theological disputes among Christians themselves, as there are also among the various Muslim schools of thought.

Conclusion

We would like to stress how much Catholics and Muslims share: belief in One God, who created the universe out of love; the conviction that the center of religious life is submission and obedience to the will of God; and the confidence that God's will is a transforming power that can renew individual and social life in every aspect. Through dialogue and improved cooperation, Muslims and Catholics can develop a just and peaceful society in the spirit of the teachings of the Gospel and the Qur'ān. Both Jesus and Muhammad loved and cared for all whom they met, especially the poor and oppressed; their teachings and example call for solidarity with the poor, oppressed, homeless, hungry, and needy in today's world.

This text is only one step in a theological dialogue between Catholics and Muslims. As a result, we hope that this resource is instructive for those who make use of it and that it will be an encouragement for more dialogue and sharing between Catholics and Muslims. We firmly believe that God calls us to this dialogue and blesses the efforts of those who seek to do the will of God.

References

Al-Bukhārī, Muhammad Ibn Ismī'īl. *The Translation of the Meanings of Sahīh al-Bukhārī: Arabic-English.* Volume 1. Translated by Muhammad Muhsin Khan. Chicago: Kazi Publications, 1979.

Basil the Great. *On the Holy Spirit.* Translated with introduction by David Anderson. Crestwood, NY: St. Vladimir's Seminary Press, 1980.

Bonaventure. *Bonaventure: The Soul's Journey into God, The Tree of Life, The Life of St. Francis.* Translated with introduction by Ewert Cousins. New York: Paulist, 1979.

Denzinger, Henry, and Adolfus Schönmetzer, eds. *Enchiridion Symbolorum: Definitionum et Declarationum de Rebus Fidei et Morum.* 23rd ed. Freiburg: Herder, 1965.

First Vatican Council. *Dei Filius (Dogmatic Constitution on the Catholic Faith).* In Denzinger-Schönmetzer.

Flannery, Austin, ed. *Vatican Council II: Vol. 1: The Conciliar and Post Conciliar Documents.* Northport, NY: Costello, 1996.

Second Vatican Council. *Dei Verbum* (DV) *(Dogmatic Constitution on Divine Revelation).* In Flannery.

Second Vatican Council. *Lumen Gentium* (LG) *(Dogmatic Constitution on the Church).* In Flannery.

Second Vatican Council. *Sacrosanctum Concilium* (SC) *(Constitution on the Sacred Liturgy).* In Flannery.

Participants

The Midwest Dialogue of Catholics and Muslims began meeting in October 1996 and reconvened every autumn for the next seven years. Those who were able to attend the October 2003 meeting reviewed a draft of the preface, introduction, and three chapters of text that would eventually be edited and published under the title *Revelation: Catholic and Muslim Perspectives*. After the 2003 meeting, certain members of the dialogue prepared revisions drawing from the discussion that year among the participants and from additional suggestions from the members and sponsors of the dialogue.

Those who have participated as members of the dialogue are on the list below. A few on this list participated in all eight meetings from 1996 to 2003. About a quarter attended seven or eight meetings, and most attended at least half the meetings. This dialogue was an ongoing enterprise overseen and facilitated by members and staff of the sponsoring organizations, the Islamic Society of North America and the United States Conference of Catholic Bishops.

Dr. Ghulam-Haider Aasi, *American Islamic College, Chicago, IL*
Sheikh Muhammad Nur Abdullah, *Dar-ul-Islam Masjid, St. Louis, MO*
Imam Farooq Aboelzahab, *Islamic Center of Greater Toledo, Perrysburg, OH*
Mr. Mustafa Acar, *Purdue University, West Lafayette, IN*
Mr. Muktar Ahmad, *Islamic Society of North America, Plainfield, IN*
Imam Fajri Ansari, *Masjid Nu`Man, Buffalo, NY*
Dr. Shahid Athar, *Indianapolis, IN*
Dr. John Borelli, *U. S. Conference of Catholic Bishops, Washington, D.C.*
Bishop Kevin M. Britt, *Diocese of Grand Rapids, MI*
Archbishop Alexander J. Brunett, *Archdiocese of Seattle, WA*
Fr. David Bruning, *Diocese of Toledo, OH*
Fr. John G. Budde, *Archdiocese of Detroit, MI*
Fr. David Burrell, CSC, *University of Notre Dame, IN*
Dr. Assad Busool, *American Islamic College, Chicago, IL*
Imam Fawaz Damra, *Islamic Center of Cleveland, Cleveland, OH*
Imam Mohammad Ali Elahi, *Islamic House of Wisdom, Dearborn Heights, MI*
Mr. Ahmed El-Hattab, *Islamic Society of North America, Plainfield, IN*
Mr. Khalid M. Eltom, *Kokomo, IN*
Sr. Mary Margaret Funk, OSB, *Our Lady of Grace Monastery, Beech Grove, IN*
Fr. William Hammer, *Archdiocese of Louisville, KY*

Fr. Vincent A. Heier, *Archdiocese of St. Louis, MO*
Fr. Joseph Hilinski, Diocese of Cleveland, OH
Imam A. M. Khattab, *Islamic Center of Greater Toledo, Perrysburg, OH*
Mr. Arif Jalil, *Kokomo, IN*
Dr. Irfan Ahmad Khan, *Markam, IL*
Sheikh Mohammed Amin Kholwadia, *Glendale Heights, IL*
Fr. Leo D. Lefebure, *Fordham University, Bronx, NY*
Dr. M. Iqbal Malik, *Carmel, IN*
Fr. Elias D. Mallon, SA, *Friars of the Atonement, NY*
Imam Adel Marzouk, *Islamic Society of North America, Plainfield, IN*
Fr. Francis X. Mazur, *Diocese of Buffalo, NY*
Sr. Joan Monica McGuire, OP, *Archdiocese of Chicago, IL*
Fr. Thomas Michel, SJ, *Jesuit Curia, Vatican City*
Fr. Thomas Murphy, *Archdiocese of Indianapolis, IN*
Dr. Thomas Ryba, *St. Thomas Aquinas Center, Purdue University, West Lafayette, IN*
Imam Michael Saahir, *Nur-Allah Islamic Center, Indianapolis, IN*
Dr. Ghouse A. Shareef and Mrs. Sameena D. Shareef, *Louisville, KY*
Imam Muhammad Siddeeq, *Indianapolis, IN*
Dr. Sayyid M. Syeed, *Islamic Society of North America, Plainfield, IN*
Ms. Rita George Tvrtkovic, *Archdiocese of Chicago, IL*
Fr. John West, *Archdiocese of Detroit, MI*
Fr. Jude D. Weisenbeck, *Archdiocese of Louisville, KY*
Mr. David R. Wilson, *Diocese of Lafayette, IN*